T0318625

Cambridge Elements ≡

Elements in Public Policy
edited by
M. Ramesh
National University of Singapore
Michael Howlett
Simon Fraser University, British Colombia
David L. Weimer
University of Wisconsin – Madison
Xun Wu
Hong Kong University of Science and Technology
Judith Clifton
University of Cantabria
Eduardo Araral
National University of Singapore

THE PROTECTIVE STATE

Christopher Ansell
University of California, Berkeley

CAMBRIDGE
UNIVERSITY PRESS

CAMBRIDGE
UNIVERSITY PRESS

University Printing House, Cambridge CB2 8BS, United Kingdom

One Liberty Plaza, 20th Floor, New York, NY 10006, USA

477 Williamstown Road, Port Melbourne, VIC 3207, Australia

314–321, 3rd Floor, Plot 3, Splendor Forum, Jasola District Centre,
New Delhi – 110025, India

79 Anson Road, #06–04/06, Singapore 079906

Cambridge University Press is part of the University of Cambridge.

It furthers the University's mission by disseminating knowledge in the pursuit of
education, learning, and research at the highest international levels of excellence.

www.cambridge.org
Information on this title: www.cambridge.org/9781108739610
DOI: 10.1017/9781108667081

© Christopher Ansell 2019

First published 2019

A catalogue record for this publication is available from the British Library.

ISBN 978-1-108-73961-0 Paperback
ISSN 2398-4058 (online)
ISSN 2514-3565 (print)

The Protective State

Elements in Public Policy

DOI: 10.1017/9781108667081
First published online: April 2019

Christopher Ansell
University of California, Berkeley

Author for correspondence: Christopher Ansell cansell@berkeley.edu

Abstract: The modern state protects citizens from many different harms, from industrial accidents to airline crashes. This Element illuminates a distinctive politics of protection that transcends policy sectors as diverse as criminal justice, consumer protection, and public health. Adopting a comparative and historical perspective, the Element identifies common drivers of protective state building as well as cross-national differences in the politics of protection. The Element concludes by examining political theories of the protective state, which seek to defend and critique the obligations for and the limits of state protection.

Keywords: protection

ISBNs: 9781108739610 (PB), 9781108667081 (OC)
ISSNs: 2398-4058 (online), 2514-3565 (print)

Contents

The OFFICE of the Soveraign, (be it a Monarch, or an Assembly,) consisteth in the end, for which he was trusted with the Soveraign Power, namely the procuration of the Safety Of The People

— Thomas Hobbes, *Leviathan* (1651)

1 Thou Shalt Protect?

The state protects citizens from many different harms. This protective role can be traced back before the origins of the modern state, but it has changed dramatically over the past half century, becoming more extensive, elaborate, and politically contested. "People depend on government regulation," writes the legal scholar Jack Beermann, "to ensure the safety of virtually every human activity" (2015, 303). In addition to traditional areas of protection (crime, disease, and military security), the protective state now protects wives from husbands and children from parents. It protects investors, consumers, data, and endangered species, and we hope it protects us from suicide bombers, carcinogens, and cyberbullies.

This protective role is at the heart of an implicit social contract between state and society. Citizens expect protection. As a British citizen complained after the 2007 floods: "I started to feel quite angry ... because I think their job is to protect citizens and I just feel they didn't do that."[1] Woe be to the public official who ignores this social contract, as Korean President Park Geun-hye learned when the Korean legislature sought to impeach her for failing "to protect citizens' lives" (Sang-Hun 2016). The protective state even extends to international politics where an international doctrine known as "responsibility to protect" requires states to proactively intervene to protect citizens of other states from genocide or humanitarian disaster (Bellamy 2010).

According to the *Oxford English Dictionary*, "protect" means "to defend or guard from danger or injury." Yet the state's protective role is not limited to protecting people from physical harm. The state protects property and property rights, a role expanded in recent years to encompass minority shareholders (Guillén and Capron 2016), critical infrastructures (Aradau 2010), and data (Bennett 1988). States also extend protection to animals and the environment (Nash 1989; Otto 2005). Understanding the scope and character of protections afforded by the state provides an important insight into the state itself and the process of state building.

Extensive scholarship exists about the welfare state, the regulatory state, the developmental state, the security state, and even the green state, but the protective state is scarcely recognized as a distinctive idea (cf. Béland 2005).

---

[1] Quoted in Butler and Pidgeon 2011, 543.

Specialized literatures exist on crime control, terrorism, crisis management, natural hazards, humanitarian emergencies, social protection, environmental protection, and consumer protection – each observing the protective state in one of its many guises. But this specialization makes it easy to miss the wider dynamics of the protective state. Even in the face of pressures to retrench welfare states and deregulate the economy, democratic states have often expanded or elaborated their protective role.

While the "welfare state" and the "protective state" are overlapping concepts, they also diverge in important respects. The welfare state provides "social protection" to individuals and families in the face of the vagaries of the labor market. It relies extensively, though not exclusively, on redistribution to provide well-being or security to broad categories of citizens – an ambit running from "means-tested" to "universal" provision of services. The protective state seeks to protect against *discrete harms, accidents, hazards, threats, and risks* – a job-related accident, a terrorist attack, a disease outbreak, a case of consumer fraud, or a devastating flood (Sparrow 2008).[2] These potential harms are often understood to be exceptional in nature, produced by breakdowns of the normal social order, institutional failures, market externalities, or unintended consequences. Responses range from "reactive" to "preventive," and the policy instruments of choice are often regulatory and coercive.

Demands for state protection cross partisan lines. While the left tends to be more concerned about protecting citizens from the market and corporate power, the right prioritizes harms that threaten or result from social disorder and national security. Still, as the protective state has become more elaborate and extensive, its protective role has become more politically contested. In the United States, for example, consumer and environmental mobilization in the 1960s and 1970s was met by a corporate backlash against consumer and environmental protection in the 1980s and 1990s (Switzer and Vaughn 1997; Hilton 2009, 154–184). Although expectations of state protection often cross partisan lines, many policy sectors associated with protection have become politicized – from occupational safety (Dingwall and Frost 2017) to food safety (Nestle 2013) to flood control (Tarlock 2012).

The state's protective role is often fraught with moral ambiguity. As political theorist Wendy Brown writes, "Whether one is dealing with the state, the Mafia, parents, pimps, police, or husbands, the heavy price of institutionalized protection is always a measure of dependence and agreement to abide by the protector's rule" (Brown 1995, 169). To protect citizens from terrorism, the protective

---

[2] For a discussion of the meaning of "protection" in the context of refugee protection, see Storey (2016).

state may normalize emergency powers that infringe on civil liberties (Agamben 2005; Tsoukala 2006). To protect children from abuse, the state must intrude into the private lives of families (Donzelot 1977). Anti-vaccine activists and climate-change deniers reject the need for state protection and the "nanny state" epithet is frequently brandished (Moore, Yeatman, and Davey 2015). Others express outrage when the state fails to protect. After a series of devastating wildfires in his state, Washington Governor Jay Inslee skewered the Trump administration for its failure to take climate change seriously: "There is anger in my state about the administration's failure to protect us," he said, "When you taste it on your tongue, it's a reality" (Inslee quoted in Eilperin, Dennis, and Mooney 2018).

Why a focus on the *state* when other scholars speak of "risk society," "risk regulation," or "societal security"? The reason is not that society or non-state institutions are unimportant. On the contrary, the changing protective role of the state is a barometer of public demand for protection and for whom it holds responsible to provide it. The term "state" is used here to signify all the democratic and authoritative institutions of modern government, including legislative, executive, and judicial branches. The term "protective state" signals that the political dynamics of protection are not limited to any single branch of government or to any particular mode of governing like regulation, social services, or security.

As an analytical concept, the protective state is meant to illuminate how protection serves as a basic source of political legitimation. It also draws attention to the increasing salience of protection as a logic of governing, capturing what criminologist David Garland describes as "a new and urgent emphasis upon the need for security, the containment of danger, the identification and management of any kind of risk" (2001, 12). It also offers a lens for understanding a range of trends and developments that fall between or cut across traditional analytical categories like social welfare, public health, consumer protection, criminal justice, or international security. The point of this Element is neither to suggest that the state coddles its citizens nor to decry its failures to provide adequate protection. Instead, the mission is to explore the political and institutional dynamics that arise around the state's protective role. Three broad features of protective state politics are noted at the outset – its debates about prevention, its focus on risk, and its tendency to securitize issues.

1.1 Prevention versus Reaction

While scholars judge the welfare state in terms of how "universal" (or decommodified) versus "residual" (e.g., means tested) it is, the protective state is judged by how preventive versus reactive it is. Although the public may only expect compensation and relief after an injurious event has occurred (Friedman and Thompson 2003), it often expects the state to *prevent* accidents and disasters from happening in the first place. In part, this shift toward prevention represents changing perceptions about the causes of harm. For example, the meaning of "accident" has changed over time from an event that is unavoidable to something that can be prevented (Green 1997). Some scholars argue that the concept of "protection" entails prevention (Parton 2008, 174; Peeters 2015; Pratt and Anderson 2015).

This preventive focus also partly reflects expectations about the capacity to control harms. From a modernist perspective, the sociologist Raymond Lau observes, "all mishaps are seen as preventable" (2009, 668). Indeed, science provides a powerful resource for advocacy groups to demand more preventive policy. For example, the late-twentieth-century preventive approaches to alcoholism and smoking were influenced both by new modes of political mobilization (via groups like MADD or GASP, respectively) and new science about fetal alcohol syndrome and secondhand smoke (Brown and Fee 2014).

The public health community has traditionally argued for prevention strategies (Atwood, Colditz, and Kawachi 1997). However, a distinctive feature of the protective state is that this preventive approach is extended to policy domains like criminal justice that have traditionally been more reactive (Garland 2001; Harris 2005; Janus 2006; Welsh, Braga, and Sullivan 2014). In the Netherlands, for instance, a turn to preventive crime policy occurred in the mid-1980s (Peeters 2015). Prevention has also been linked to the expansion of surveillance as a mode of governance (Balkin 2008; Parton 2008, 2010) and to the contemporary desire to enhance resilience (O'Malley 2010).

The politics of the protective state tend to become structured along a reactive-preventive dimension. The limits of a reactive approach often become the basis for arguing for more preventive action. The legal scholar David Friedman, for example, criticizes US protection of consumers against fraud as "a sprawling, reactive consumer protection regime that fails to fully address this important social and economic problem" (2007, 46). To protect consumers, he argues, the United States needs to move to a deterrence strategy.

Tragedies and disasters are often framed as failures of the state to take adequate precautions or to act in a timely fashion. After several high-profile tragedies, for example, the UK's 1989 Child Protection Act placed a strong emphasis on prevention, creating what the social welfare scholar Nigel Parton has called the "preventive-surveillance state" (Parton 2008; see also France and Utting 2005). Even after a policy regime has moved toward prevention, subsequent failure can reinforce demands for preventive action. As a study of crime prevention succinctly puts it: "In reaction to failed prevention, more prevention is proposed" (Peeters 2013, 21).

1.2 Risk

A second prominent feature of the protective state is its expanding focus on risk and increasing contestation about how to respond to it (Moss 2004; Aradau, Lobo-Guerrero, and Van Munster 2008; Ewald 2014). Regulation scholar David Moss has written that "[r]isk management policies have now proliferated to such an extent that is hard to think of any greater governmental responsibility" (2004, 2). By the 1980s, risk assessment had come to play a powerful but disputed role in regulatory decision making and in criminal justice (Feeley and Simon 1992; Simon 2005; Lofstedt 2011; Nash 2017).

The protective state does not simply protect against risk. It also uses risk as a governing technique. One view of the rise of risk management is that it helps to rationalize demands upon the state and limit the fallout from failures to protect (Rothstein, Huber, and Gaskell 2006). For instance, the Japanese have adopted a risk-based system to move away from the perception that food safety can be "zero risk" (Yamaguchi 2014). Risk-based regulation has also developed in Europe and North America, though it has been taken up somewhat more readily in the UK and the United States than in Germany, France, or Denmark (Lodge and Wegrich 2011; Krieger 2013; Rothstein, Borraz, and Huber 2013; Almond and Esbester 2018).

While risk assessment and management have expanded, so have criticisms of their ability to address uncertainty (Klinke and Renn 2002; O'Malley 2004; Loftsted 2011; Vogel 2012; Hardy and Maguire 2016). One argument is that greater public and scientific concern about uncertainty and the irreversibility of consequences has reinforced a precautionary approach to risk (Ewald 1999; Hebenton and Seddon 2009; Boschen et al. 2010). A criticism of the precautionary approach is that it leads to "worst case" or "possibilistic" thinking that can in turn lead to the overestimation of threats (Sunstein 2005; Clarke 2006; Furedi 2009; Amoore 2013). While critics of market and technological externalities are often favorable toward a precautionary approach, it is important to point out that the appeal of precaution cuts across left-right divisions. Just as the left advances precaution against biotechnology, President Trump seeks a ban on Muslim immigration in the name of precaution. A precautionary logic can be used to prevent exposure to toxic chemicals (Vogel 2012) or to exert preventive control over those who have already served time for a sexual crime (Hebenton and Seddon 2009).

A central theme of the protective state is "who bears the risk?" – a theme often linked to debates about whether risk is an individual or a collective responsibility (Mascini, Achterberg, and Houtman 2013). The consumer movements of the 1960s and 1970s, for example, sought to shift risk from consumers to producers (Trumbull 2006). A prominent theme in the recent literature on risk is that neoliberalism has sought to shift risk back onto citizens through its emphasis on "responsibilization" and "resilience" (Gray 2009; Joseph 2013; Hutter, Leibenath, and Mattissek 2014; cf. Lau 2009; Collier 2014; Demeritt et al. 2015).

1.3 Security and Securitization

Broadly speaking, we can understand security as a response to an existential threat – traditionally, a military threat (Balzacq 2008). However, if "threat" is understood broadly as a *potential but intentional harm*, we then come to appreciate that security is not limited to military threats and may be more generic. The international relations literature refers to the process of extending the logic of security to issues beyond military security as "securitization" (Wæver 1995).

The politics of the protective state tend to widen the scope of securitization, raising questions about which problems and risks will be brought under the security umbrella. Will risks like climate change, drugs, infectious diseases, or food-borne pathogens be conceived as security threats to a state or nation? The answer to this question has important consequences because securitization is often understood to bestow an exceptional quality on the state's response and to focus attention on prevention of the threat. For example, after the September 11 attacks, the idea of airline "safety" was trumped by the concept of airline "security" (Cobb and Primo 2003). In other words, preventing terrorist threats to airlines was given priority over the conventional concern with the safety of airline technology and operations.

Infectious disease response is a prominent example of the expanding scope of securitization, particularly at the global level (Abraham 2011; Elbe 2012; Kamradt-Scott 2012; Hanrieder and Kreuder-Sonnen 2014). Abraham (2011) describes a securitization of disease that begins with AIDS but is pushed along by the anthrax attacks and the SARS epidemic and fears about the weaponization of smallpox. Elbe (2012) argues that the securitization of disease depends on a shift in focus from protecting the territory of the state to protecting the welfare of the population.

Elements of securitization can also be seen as operating in domestic disasters like flooding (Wood 2016) and in ideas like "homeland security" or "societal security" that cut across a range of hazards (hence, the concept "all hazards"), blurring distinctions between safety and security (Collier and Lakoff 2008; Lango, Rykkja, and Lægreid 2011). Some scholars have pointed to the outlines of a "security state" that blur the lines between crime control and warfare

(Andreas and Price 2001; Hallsworth and Lea 2011) and between internal and external security (Bigo 2006). Others point to the expansion of surveillance as an indicator of the wider securitization of the state (Balkin 2008; cf. Kerr 2009).

1.4 The Scope of the Element

The goal of this Element is to bring many strands of argument together in a synthetic fashion to illuminate a many-sided phenomenon – the protective state. To do so, the Element draws synthetically from a diverse range of protective issues – child protection, flooding, violence against women, human trafficking, workplace safety, toxic chemicals, infectious disease, food safety, sex offenses, and terrorism, among others. To keep the task manageable, the scope of the investigation is limited in a number of important ways. No attempt is made to judge whether the state's protective role is good or bad or to evaluate how well or how equitably we are ultimately protected. The scope of the argument is also limited to democratic nations with highly developed economies. Authoritarian states and less-developed nations may also protect their citizens, but the social and political dynamics may be quite different. The international dimension of the protective state is also a topic primarily left for future research.

The next four sections of the Element elaborate this argument about the protective state. Section 2 puts the development of the protective state in a state-building perspective, focusing on the major developments that have molded the contemporary transformation of the protective state. Section 3 explores the political dynamics of the protective state, examining some of the characteristic ways that demands for protection get mobilized and organized. Section 4 adopts a comparative perspective to illuminate national differences in protection. Finally, Section 5 explores the "political theory" of the protective state, investigating some of the normative issues that arise in justifying and appraising the state's protective role.

2 The Rise of the Protective State

The state's protective role is as old – indeed older – than modern nation-states. The first English King Henry ruled in the twelfth century that masters were responsible for the workplace injuries of their apprentices (Leka et al. 2017). Holland built defenses against floods as early as the thirteenth century, and Venice introduced quarantines to protect the city from the plague early in the fifteenth century. States have protected their "citizens" from foreign invaders or from their neighbors since well before the consolidation of the modern state system (Tilly 1985). Indeed, the developmental path of the protective state basically follows the trajectory of state building. As states extended their geographical reach and control, as they developed a regularized administrative machinery to deliver services, as the sense of the state as a nation was consolidated, and as democratic modes of political contestation were institutionalized, so too was the protective role of the state elaborated, expanded, and constrained.

The first modern wave of protective state building occurred in the last third of the nineteenth century and the first decade of the twentieth century – broadly speaking, the Progressive Era in the United States, the Third Republic in France, Wilhelmine Germany, Victorian Britain, and so on. Before this period, the state's protective role was primarily focused on preventing foreign invasion, maintaining public order, and to some extent safeguarding public health. These traditional protective functions were consolidated and expanded at the end of the nineteenth century: militaries expanded and professionalized (Skowronek 1982), police forces expanded and began to specialize in crime control (Monkkonen 1992), and a "sanitation revolution" led the state to expand its role in disease prevention (Duffy 1992; Porter 1999).

The late-nineteenth-century state also expanded into new areas of protection – notably, into "protective" legislation regulating the conditions of labor, often with a special focus on protecting women and children (Urofsky 1985; Feurer 1988; Jenson 1989; Skocpol 1992; Wikander, Kessler-Harris, and Lewis 1995; Woloch 2015). Protection of consumers – qua consumers – also began to expand in the late nineteenth century (Hilton 2009) and early attempts to protect children and animals from abuse were developed (Pfohl 1977; Kete 2002; Myers 2008). The mobilization of women, consumers, public health, and labor acted in various ways to support this expansion.

A second wave of organizing occurred in the 1930s and 1940s, consolidating and extending the incipient protections developed at the turn of the century. For example, in the United States, the New Deal expanded the state's role in protecting women workers (Novkov 2001), strengthened the state's role in food safety (Thomas 2014) and aviation safety (O'Neil and Krane 2012), and took new steps to protect consumers (Glickman 2001). In a speech in 1937, a prominent proponent of the New Deal administrative state, Securities and Exchange Commission Chairman David Landis, described how regulatory institutions ensured "the security of our bank deposits, the safety of our life insurance, our protection against fraud and chicanery in the sale of securities, our necessity for having light and power at reasonable rates, our protection against discrimination in railroad tariffs, or as workmen, our protection against unfair discrimination in employment or our right to compensation for industrial accident" (Landis quoted in Wang 2005, 273–4). The New Deal also sought to greatly expand the state's role in security by creating the now mostly forgotten Federal Security Agency (FSA) (Cuéllar 2009). Not to be confused with the National Security Agency (NSA), the FSA broadened the state's security umbrella to a range of domestic issues. World War II also expanded the state's domestic emergency response capacity (Roberts 2013; Curley 2015).

A third wave of protective state building began in the 1960s and 1970s. Although welfare state expansion occurred throughout the postwar period, a wave of legislative developments in the 1960s and 1970s expanded and consolidated consumer and environmental protection (Keiser 1980; Sunstein 2002b; Vogel 2003; Trumbull 2006). New developments occurred in occupational safety (Kelman 1981; Wilson 1985), automotive safety (Lee 1998), child protection (Myers 2008; Dekker 2010), teenage pregnancy (Linders and Bogard 2014), domestic violence (Elman 1996; Sack 2004), workplace discrimination (Pedriana 2006), sexual harassment (Saguy 2000), aviation security (more in Europe; Hainmüller and Lemnitzer 2003), and data protection (Bennett 1988). Writing of the United States, Bardach and Kagan observe, "In the 1960s and 1970s, a quantum leap seems to have been taken in legislator's eagerness to provide this kind of extra protection" (2002, 11; see also Shapiro and Glicksman 2003).

Although it is hard to distinguish the most recent wave of protective state developments from the third wave, a series of events beginning in the mid-1980s – the AIDS crisis, "mad cow" disease, the SARS epidemic, Hurricane Katrina, and the September 11 terrorist attacks – arguably triggered the most recent set of developments in the protective state. In the United States, welfare state retrenchment and deregulatory pressures beginning in the 1980s placed significant constraints on the further development of the protective state, even as a European Union regulatory state responsible for a wide range of protections began to develop rapidly at the end of the 1990s (Majone 1994, 1997; Vogel 2003, 2012). Still, even in the United States, concerns related to infectious diseases, food safety, natural hazards, human trafficking, public safety, and terrorism were highly prominent. Examples of new or extended realms of protection on both sides of the Atlantic include critical infrastructure protection (Aradau 2010; Collier and Lakoff 2015), patient safety (Small and Barach 2002), aviation security (more in the United States; Hainmüller and Lemnitzer 2003), disability rights (Heyer 2002), elder abuse and neglect (Penhale 2007), human trafficking (Friesendorf 2007; Weitzer 2007), "dangerous dogs" (Lodge and Hood 2002), dietary supplements (Dickens 2014; Binns, Lee, and Lee 2018), and sexual predators (Janus 2006).

The point of describing these waves of protective state expansion and elaboration is not to argue that each wave was independent. To some extent, each wave built on political and institutional developments in prior waves. In many cases, new developments responded to perceived gaps or failures of protective legislation or programs developed in prior waves. For example, in US drug safety, the 1938 Food, Drug and Cosmetics Act expanded the scope and powers of the federal government set out in the Pure Food and Drugs Act of 1906 (Daemmrich 2004; Carpenter and Sin 2007). The Kefauver-Harris Amendments of 1962 then expanded the scope of regulatory powers established by the 1938 act (Temin 1985; Daemmrich 2004). A wave metaphor does have a tendency, however, to gloss over incremental legal and programmatic changes and to underestimate the counter-mobilization that pushes back against expanded protections.

The advantage of the wave metaphor is that it helps us perceive cross-sectoral dynamics. As these four waves suggest, the expansion of the protective state often cuts across different policy sectors. Although state protections are typically instantiated in particular sectoral policies or programs (food safety, human trafficking, etc.), state protection often expands in a more *general* fashion, affecting several sectors at once.

2.1 The Contemporary Transformation of the Protective State

In the mid-1980s, the sociologist Ulrich Beck (1992) made the provocative argument that a "risk society" was replacing "industrial society." In this new society, concerns about the consequences of risk were magnified and fell on rich and poor alike. In Beck's memorable phrase, "poverty is hierarchic, smog is democratic" (1992, 36). People were now bound together by a "commonality of anxiety" rather than a "commonality of need" (1992, 49). As a result, the ethical rationale of society shifted from equality to safety, and the risk society became oriented toward the future and the potential for harms. As Anthony Giddens later wrote of the risk society, "it is a society increasingly preoccupied with the future (and also with safety), which generates the notion of risk" (1999, 3).

Despite Beck's prescience, his argument is too sweeping to capture the many interacting factors that have transformed the protective state. The remainder of this section examines these interacting factors in greater detail.

2.2 Rising Expectations and Loss of Control

The contemporary protective state is born of the paradoxical tensions between rising expectations about being protected and the fear, anxiety, and distrust that comes with personal loss of control over protection. On the one hand, the postwar period was a time of rising affluence and educational expansion, where science, technology, organizations, and markets bestowed unparalleled capacities for control (Flickinger 1983; Beniger 2009).[3] These dazzling achievements naturally ramped up expectations about what could and should be controlled (Friedman 1994). On the other hand, our mastery of nature has led us to take greater risks (Knowles 2012), creating "manufactured risks" with more catastrophic potential (Giddens 1999, 4; see also Beck 1992). Moreover, science, technology, organizations, and markets can limit our capacity to unilaterally control our own fate. The modern world expands our expectations of control while eroding our sense of unilateral or local control.[4]

Food exemplifies these tensions and trade-offs. Our food supply once depended on subsistence farming and the vagaries of nature. Now we walk into a grocery store and buy the potatoes and asparagus we want regardless of the season. Technology, organizations, and markets combine to guarantee an abundant and reliable food supply – an incredible achievement of control. The trade-off is that we no longer personally control our food supply. Instead, it comes from distant farms, is highly processed, and is subject to food safety failures far beyond our control. As the food historian Harvey Levenstein writes, "the erosion of the reassuring personal relationships between sellers and buyers made [Americans] particularly susceptible to food scares" (2012, 3). When you raise your own food, you control your own risk. When far-flung supply chains produce food, you depend on them to guarantee the safety of your food (Levenstein 2012; Sheingate 2012).

On one side of the ledger sheet, our success produces expectations that collective control over risk is possible. As Beck writes, "Where everything has become controllable, the product of human efforts, the age of excuses is over" (1992, 234). On the other side of the ledger, the fear and anxiety that come with our loss of individual control often convince us that protection is necessary. A paradoxical result is what has been called the "fail safe" society (Piller 1991) where there is "a myth that accidents should not happen" (Green 1997, 149). In their study of US regulatory expansion, Bardach and Kagan suggest that "cultural changes in the past two decades have increased our *intolerance of risk*, resulting in greater expectations of security from physical hazards, illness, environmental degradation, and even from begin cheated in the marketplace" (2002, 12, emphasis in original).

---

[3] As Hilton writes, "organized consumerism developed in those countries where an expanding middle class bought more of the luxury and semi-luxury items associated with the age of affluence: cars, refrigerators, televisions, stereos, washing machines, vacuum cleaners" (2009, 25).

[4] A well-developed body of research finds that the controllability of risk affects people's perception of risk (e.g., Slovic, Fischhoff, and Lichtenstein 1986; Sjöberg 2000).

Citizen fear and anxiety about risks is one of the driving factors of the development of the protective state. Scholars argue that a "culture of fear" began in the 1970s and expanded in the 1980s and 1990s (Glassner 1999; Furedi 2005; Gourevitch 2010; Wuthnow 2010; Critcher 2011; Spicer and Bowen 2016). This culture or politics of fear can encourage crisis-driven or panic-driven policy making (Glassner 1999) or "moral panics" (Walker 2010) that may stem from any number of specific anxieties – youth wearing "hoodies" in the UK (Hier et al. 2011), the welfare state (Shepard 2007), drug use (Jenkins 1994), pandemics (Caduff 2015), or sexual predators (Huffman 2016). The politicization of science – and the uncertainty it raises – may also increase public anxiety about threats (Bolsen and Druckman 2015).

Studies show an overall worldwide increase in anxiety between 1970 and 2010 (Booth, Sharma, and Leader 2016) and find support for the argument that anxiety leads citizens to support protective policies (Albertson and Gadarian 2015). Fear and anxiety also lead to more punitive crime prevention policies (Garland 2001; Brown and Socia 2016) and, arguably, disproportionate demands for protection. For example, cyberterrorism "aggravates stress and anxiety, intensifies feelings of vulnerability and hardens political attitudes" (Gross, Canetti, and Vashdi 2017, 49) and fears about terrorism lead Americans "to demand too much homeland security" (Friedman 2011, 77).

2.3 The Policy State and the Expanding Role of Science

A very broad factor in the rise of a protective state is the major expansion of the "policy state" in the second half of the twentieth century (Skowronek 2009; Patashnik and Zelizer 2013; Rocco 2015). By creating policies and programs, the policy state can institutionalize concern about protecting citizens (Wuthnow 2010). Furthermore, by extending surveillance, funding research, or collecting statistics, the policy state may increase concern about some risks and reveal new risks (Dunn 2007). Entrepreneurial agencies may work with social movements and advocacy groups to expand certain protections (Carpenter 2001; Weldon and Htun 2013). In the United States, for example, tobacco control has expanded through an alliance between the National Cancer Institute and local anti-smoking campaigns (Studlar 2014).

As the policy state expanded, "policy subsystems" or "policy networks" formed to control the details of policy outcomes and the timing and content of policy change (Heclo 1978; Baumgartner and Jones 1991; Marsh and Rhodes 1992). Scholars have described how these networks may be more or less open, affecting the production of public policy (Heclo 1978; Gormley 1986; Baumgartner and Jones 1991; Howlett and Ramesh 1998; Howlett 2002). In a now classic argument, Hugh Heclo (1978) suggests that the growth of the policy state leads policy subsystems to become more open and susceptible to policy innovation. A likely source of protective state expansion is that protective issues enter the policy-making agenda as closed policy networks get pried open. An expansion of advocacy beginning in the 1970s was an important driver of this process (Nownes and Neeley 1996).

Comparative studies of agricultural policy networks illustrate the point. In a study of Danish and Swedish agricultural policy networks, Daugbjerg (1998) found that the more open Swedish policy network allowed increased representation of consumers, which ultimately produced stronger environmental protection. Marsh and Smith (2000) argue that between 1945 and 1980, the UK's closed agricultural policy network subordinated consumer food safety interests to producer interests. This closed network broke down in the late 1980s due to consumer mobilization and a shift in market power from producers to retailers (Smith 1991).

The expansion of the protective state also reflects the expanding role of science in policy making (Ezrahi 1990). In a broad cultural sense, science has largely replaced religion in explaining and giving meaning to disasters (Dekker 2017). More politically, science has authority that has been woven into the fabric of governing (Jasanoff 1990, 2011). One expression of the power of science and expertise in shaping the protective state is the "medicalization" of issues, which means that the legitimacy and authority of medical science is used to rationalize problems and their solutions in medical terms (Conrad 2007). Studies describe the medicalization of a wide range of protective issues, including homelessness (Bogard 2001), domestic violence (Sweet 2015), obesity (Kersh and Morone 2002), sexual offenses (Saetta 2016), and child protection (Fangerau, Görgen, and Griemmert 2015).

Science both discovers potential harms and justifies action to prevent them, while also of course producing them (Litfin 1994). Moreover, as science and expertise have become central to protective politics, they have also become more contested, a trend that arguably accelerated in the 1990s (Joly 2007; Gauchat 2012). Sociologist Peter Weingart memorably described how the "scientization of politics" is accompanied by the "politicization of science" (1999, 151). In some cases, the depoliticization of science increases the authority of scientists to shape policy – as it did, for instance, in the case of maternal protection (Jansson 2009). However, scientists increasingly play activist roles, becoming allies of advocacy coalitions – as seen in the mobilization against toxic chemicals (Cordner, Mulcahy, and Brown, 2013).

When science and expertise are politicized – or simply distrusted – pressures to open up and democratize technocratic decision making arise (Beck 1992). The opening up of policy networks and technocratic decision making may in fact interact and be related to the politicization of science and expertise. In the 1990s, for example, France opened up its closed technocratic decision making by encouraging a "cross-examination" model of science that sets up opposing expert perspectives (Joly 2007).

2.4 Rights and Changing Social Structure

Another source of the protective state has been a "rights revolution." This revolution is sometimes understood to be a particularly American phenomenon. As Landy and Levin have written of the US context, "[t]he expansion of the concept of rights to apply to an ever more diverse array of issues and problems is the core of the new constitutional order that animates the new politics of public policy" (1995, 295). This "new politics" changes the claims that can be made about public problems. For example, pollution standards that avoid cost considerations can be defended in part by claiming that a healthy environment is a human right (Landy 1995; Nash 2017). Rights claims have led to domestic program expansion in a range of areas of protection from playground safety (Epp 2010) to data protection (Cate 1994) to disability rights (Heyer 2002).

While often understood as particularly American, the expansion of rights has a firm footing in other countries as well (Epp 1998; Berg and Geyer 2002; Skrentny 2002; Ignatieff 2007). Indeed, the rights revolution is an international phenomenon that originally grew out of a concern with protecting ethnic minorities. Human rights became a "universal language" after World War II, though some scholars argue that the concept of human rights was only consolidated in the 1970s (see Pendas 2012). Globalization deepened concerns about human rights in the 1980s (Iriye, Goedde, and Hitchcock 2012), and a new wave of international rights activism expanded the agenda for "health rights, women's rights, economic justice, and indigenous people's rights" (Cmeil 2004, 130). Consumer and environmental protections have expanded internationally through a strategy of mobilizing rights to safe products and a clean environment (Hilton 2009; Boyd 2011; Shelton, 2015).

The interaction between changing family, gender, and sexual roles and the rights revolution also led to the extension of new rights to women, children, and the LGBT community. Until the 1970s, for example, the issue of domestic violence was generally understood to be a private matter between a husband and wife. Police treaded carefully in this terrain and rarely made arrests (Sack 2004; Charles and Mackay 2013). Pushed by advocates for "battered women," state legislatures in the United States began providing the legal basis for civil protection in the mid-to-late 1970s and all US states had such laws by the early 1990s. Similar developments occurred in Europe (Hearn et al., 2016).

While these developments are understood to be "progressive" – in that they extend rights to the previously unprotected – shifts in family and community have also led to less progressive responses. Criminologists argue that more punitive attitudes toward crime grew out of the weakening of informal social controls in neighborhoods (Garland 2001) and find that citizens concerned about threats to family structure and gender relations are more likely to support punitive policies (Brown and Socia 2016). Scholars also argue that the shift from welfare to workfare accentuated anxiety among the middle class, encouraging a more punitive attitude toward crime (Wacquant 2010; Pratt and Anderson 2015).

2.5 Welfare, Regulation, and Crime

A focus on protecting citizens from *specific* harms may, in part, reflect a retrenchment of the more commodious social protections of the classic welfare state. Neil Gilbert (2002) argues that welfare states have moved away from a concept of "social citizenship," a change that has been accompanied by a relative shift from redistributive to regulatory and coercive policies (Majone 1997; Brathwaite 2000; Bardach and Kagan 2002). Meanwhile, "new social risks" have developed outside the traditional male breadwinner model of social welfare, leading to a differentiation of risks by age and status (Taylor-Gooby 2004). Indeed, it is argued that risk has replaced need as the dominant logic for allocating social protection (Kemshall 2002). Taking these arguments together, Peter Taylor-Gooby observes that a "stream of policy-related arguments presses for greater regulation of individualized life-styles" (2006, 275).

In advanced industrial nations, the regulatory state has expanded in part in response to the privatization and the deregulation of markets. Ironically, "freer markets" have led to "more rules" (Vogel 1998). However, the expansion of the protective state may also result partly from a view of the desirability of using regulatory instruments to deal with complex problems (Majone 1994, 85). In the United States, expansions of the regulatory state in the 1960s and 1970s were also associated with a rejection of tort law as the basis for providing protection (Shapiro and Glicksman 2003). Tort law was criticized as being reactive, while administrative regulation permitted the state to anticipate harms.

The combination of welfare state retrenchment and the expanding use of regulatory instruments may, in turn, be related to a greater emphasis on extending protections to individual victims and vulnerable groups. Some scholars argue that vulnerability and victimhood have become much more prominent cultural and political tropes since the 1980s (e.g., Furedi 2005). In combination with claims about rights, these tropes can provide justification for state intervention. A rights-based approach to public health, for example, regards vulnerability as an important rationale (Stephenson et al. 2014, 11). A stress on vulnerability and a stress on rights may go together in providing a justification for state protection.

Greater stress on victimhood is also a factor. As Barbara Stolz notes of the issue of human trafficking, which arose in the 1990s: "[k]ey to the reformulation of the perception of trafficking was the shift in the characterization of the trafficked person from criminal to victim" (2005, 423). This emphasis on victimization has been argued to reflect a "therapeutic culture [that] places the self at the center of the world" (Nolan 1998 15; see also Pupavac 2001; Furedi 2005). Although victims can be blamed for their victimization .and may be perceived as "whiners" (Dunn 2005), an emphasis on vulnerability and victim-hood may elevate personal security to a collective good. As David Garland observes: "the crime victim is now, in a certain sense, a representative character whose experience is assumed to be common and collective, rather than indivi-dual and atypical" (2001, 144).

What this discussion suggests is that a focus on rights, a concern with vulnerability and victimhood, and a fragmentation of social welfare around different life stages and statuses may interact to encourage specific claims for protection from a wide range of specific ills, such as hate crimes, cyberbullying, domestic violence, child abuse, consumer fraud, and human trafficking.

2.6 Consumerism

Consumer mobilization is another source of the expanding protective state. As the political scientist Gunnar Trumbull writes: "Today, arguably, no other actor in the advanced industrial countries – not the investor, not the worker, nor the welfare recipient – enjoys a more thorough set of legal and institutional protec-tions than the modern consumer when he or she enters the corner store" (2006, 2). Consumption has long been a basis for political mobilization – think of bread riots in France or the Boston Tea Party in the United States. However, scholars tend to trace contemporary consumer politics to the post–World War II era and the development of a movement to test products for their purity and authenticity (Glickman 2001; Hilton 2009). This movement developed into more broad-based consumer mobilization in the 1960s and 1970s (Trumbull 2006). President John Kennedy's 1962 Consumer Bill of Rights served as a clarion call.

Consumer protection emerged as a major political issue in the mid-1960s in the UK and the United States – in part, a political response to the challenges of inflation (Flickinger 1983; Mayer 1991). In the 1970s, consumer protection movements also expanded rapidly in France, Germany, and Sweden; in the 1980s, the EU began to make consumer protection central to its market integration agenda (Trumbull 2006). Legal protections of consumers expanded significantly in the 1960s and 1970s in Germany, France, Britain, and the United States (Hilton 2009, 52). Although consumer advocacy arguably crested in the late 1970s (Sheingate 2012), it has left behind a substantial policy legacy that continues to be periodically reactivated.

In the United States at least, and to some extent in other countries, consumerism interacted with the expansion of rights. As Landy writes, "The New Deal presided over the extension of this notion of positive rights to matters of economic security. In the 1960s and 1970s, it was expanded to encompass rights for consumers, the handicapped, and aliens, as well as environmental health" (1995, 208). Although product liability law favored producers through much of the twentieth century, consumer-oriented legal scholars and the consumer movement succeeded in partially shifting responsibility and the burden of proof onto producers during this era (Moss 2004).

2.7 Public Health

The shifting role of public health has also contributed to the transformation of the protective state. In the nineteenth century, the state's role in population health increased across urbanizing and industrializing countries, and its capacity to intervene to improve sanitation and prevent infectious diseases continued to develop throughout the twentieth century (Porter 1999; Tulchinsky and Varavikova 2014). Science and medicine played a central role in supporting and defending this expanded state role, though public health often had an uneasy alliance with clinical medicine (Duffy 1992; Niemi 2016).

To some extent, the post–World War II expansion of national health systems narrowed the role of public health. One view is that the clinical model of care embodied in these systems encouraged an "individualizing" of health, producing "an obsession with personal well-being" and an idea that health was a right of citizenship (Porter 1999, 296). The dominance of a bacteriological paradigm also led to a focus on the laboratory (Fairchild et al. 2010). The combined dominance of clinical medicine, hospitals, and laboratories eclipsed an earlier public health concern with the social determinants of health.

Several developments in public health have again broadened its scope. The bacteriological perspective that dominated medicine and public health eventually gave way to a wider concern with chronic disease. This transition was accompanied by a shift from "traditional epidemiology," with its focus on population control of infectious diseases, to "modern epidemiology" with its focus on chronic/noncommunicable disease (Pearce 1996). This new focus initially emphasized individual risk factors. However, it proved difficult to address these risk factors without taking the wider socioeconomic environment into account. Smoking, for example, was initially seen as an individual risk, but one that called for preventive policies and a wider environmental focus (Halpin, Morales-Suárez-Varela, and Martin-Moreno 2010).

In the 1970s, a movement known simply as the "New Public Health" began to break away from mid-century conceptions. Heralded by an influential 1974 Canadian report on "health promotion," the emerging paradigm was consolidated by the 1986 Ottawa Charter on Health Promotion (Fairchild et al. 2010; Tulchinsky and Varavikova 2014). The charter stressed that health promotion "undertakes action directed towards changing social, environmental, and economic conditions so as to alleviate their impact on public and individual health." The social determinants of health gained attention and the importance of advocacy in shaping effective public policy was valorized (Kickbusch 2003). The slow but expanding concern for protecting children from lead poisoning in the United States provides a good example of how this agenda has played out over time (Rosner and Markowitz 2016).

While expanding its role to include chronic disease and widening its focus to consider social and political determinants of health, public health's attitude toward infectious diseases also shifted. The sanitary revolution had partly conquered infectious diseases, but globalization and the HIV pandemic reawakened concern. In the 1980s, an influenza pandemic was not high on the international agenda, but the anthrax attacks, the SARS outbreak, and the specter of an avian flu pandemic prompted heightened attention. New fears about the possibilities of a devastating pandemic led to major new investments in pandemic preparedness (Wuthnow 2010). Global health security scholar Adam Kamradt-Scott notes, "as Western societies have become increasingly risk averse, the need for government-led interventions and protection from influenza has grown" (2012, 95). Taken together, these various developments have encouraged the public health sector to engage in a more expansive protective agenda.

2.8 Changing Security Demands, Terrorism, and Globalization

Reconfigured by the end of the Cold War, the rise of terrorism, and globalization, a new security environment has also contributed to the transformation of the protective state. The breakdown of the bipolar Cold War security logic has led to a more fluid and pluralistic situation characterized by amorphous threats and porous borders. Among the consequences of these shifts has been the securitization of a wider range of issues and an erosion of the boundary between domestic and international security. Although domestic security and international security have long been linked, particularly during war (Cuéllar 2009), global dynamics have accentuated these linkages for issues like food safety, infectious disease, human trafficking, and terrorism. While the Cold War bred its own kind of public anxiety, this post–Cold War context has created a more diffuse but no less real sense of fear.

The shift away from the systemic logic of the Cold War and the rise of terrorism may also have led to the expansion and securitization of emergency management. In the United States, for instance, Cold War emergency management was torn between a civil defense and a natural-hazards focus. After Hurricane Andrew in 1992, natural hazards were given greater attention (Roberts 2013). However, after the terrorist attack of September 11, 2001, emergency management was expanded but also subordinated to homeland security. In a review of European civil security systems, Boin et al. write, "Since the end of the Cold War and continuing between 2000 and 2012, all systems underwent considerable reform" (2014, 6).

The rising concern with terrorism interacted with globalization to expand security concerns to include a number of nontraditional areas, which in turn eroded the boundary between domestic criminal justice and external military protection. Human trafficking offers a good example of this shifting logic. Human rights groups worked hard in the 1980s and 1990s to mobilize action against trafficking. But security concerns related to international migration and transnational crime were ultimately decisive in mobilizing US support (Chuang 2006). Transnational organized crime itself became redefined as a security concern in the 1990s in both the United States and Europe (Campbell 2014).

While a tale of modernization – one that balances an optimistic view of a progressive modernity against a darker view of the ills of mass society – may appear to comfortably encompass the development of the contemporary protective state, a more in-depth investigation of the political dynamics of protection suggests a more nuanced interpretation. We now turn to an investigation of these political dynamics.

3 The Political Dynamics of the Protective State

Demands for protection often start with public appreciation that a threat of harm exists – for example, recognition that children are becoming obese, that air pollution is threatening health, or that a region is prone to superstorms. The "discovery" of a problem may reflect objective and measurable features of a phenomenon, such as laboratory tests that demonstrate the carcinogenic effects of a pesticide or rising CO_2 emissions. Yet some problems may be chronic without the public really fully noticing (Beamish 2002), and others may evoke great concern even when objective measures show a decline in significance (Linders and Bogard 2014). Clearly, more is at stake than objective conditions. Often the public only recognizes a problem when it is represented as controllable (Stone 1989) or when it has surpassed a certain threshold of attention (Wood and Doan 2003).

The framing of harms and risks is central to the politics of the protective state. A frame is a particular representation or interpretation of an issue. Frames that emphasize the systemic, societal, or environmental character of a harm or risk often provide a rationale for greater or more comprehensive state protection (Iyengar 1990; Jeon and Haider-Markel 2001; Ansell and Baur 2018). The contemporary defense of critical infrastructures, for example, grew out of a conception of "system vulnerability," which was itself a consequence of changing conceptions of war and military planning (Collier and Lakoff 2008). The debate about obesity has hinged on whether obesity is a personal or a systemic responsibility (Lawrence 2004).

Framing who is to blame or who is responsible for a hazard is often fundamental to protective state politics (Cobb and Primo 2003). As political scientist Diane Stone writes, "For the side that believes it is the victim of harm, the strongest claim it can make is to accuse someone else of intentionally causing the problem" (1989, 289). In the area of occupational health and safety, for example, the development of social insurance resulted from a shift in the framing of responsibility from worker to employer. Instead of seeing workplace accidents as the fault of careless workers, social insurance reflected the view that accidents were a product of the production system (Moss 2004). A moral framing can also be used to highlight the need for protection, as it has in the case of human trafficking (Weitzer 2007, 467).

Another framing strategy is to focus on vulnerability or victimization, with children and women often strategically framed as vulnerable and needing protection (Adler 1995; Carpenter 2005; Carpenter and Sin 2007). However, while a victim frame may be important in eliciting state protection, a victim frame may also be disempowering for the "victim," as Berns (2017) argues in the case of domestic violence.

Protective state issues are often framed in term of security, public health, or human rights – framings with different political implications and policy consequences. Securitization depends on a claim of existential threats to society and can if successful lead to greater use of military and quasi-military capacities. A public health frame often encourages (or builds on) the medicalization of issues (like obesity or child abuse) and utilizes population-level disease metaphors (obesity as an "epidemic") to justify preventive strategies. A human rights framing elevates attention to vulnerability and power and tends to emphasize victimization; it often leads to the criminalization of issues (e.g., human trafficking, domestic violence).

Issues related to harm, danger, risks, threats, or accidents do not frame themselves. An issue may have an obvious or commonsense framing, but alternative framings are often possible. Moreover, public opinion may be the ultimate arbiter of which framing of an issue will prevail. To a large degree, however, advocacy groups and policy entrepreneurs frame protective issues.

3.1 Advocacy and Policy Entrepreneurship

Advocacy mobilization is an important source of demands for state protection. Feminist mobilization, for example, is a strong cross-national predictor of the development of comprehensive policies to protect women against violence (Joachim 2003; Htun and Weldon 2012). Examples abound in other sectors as well: animal protection laws were expanded at the state level in the United States due to a concerted effort by the Humane Society (Allen 2005), and demands for specific health care protections have arisen from the proliferation of patient groups and "disease constituencies" (Epstein 2008, 2016; Keller and Packel 2014).

To mobilize support for protective state issues, advocacy groups must often mobilize support from broad, ill-defined groups. As political scientist Gunnar Trumbull writes, "The puzzle of modern consumer protection is the weakness of the political interests it protects. Consumers are by their nature disorganized: their goals are potentially diverse, the benefits of consumer protections are necessarily diffuse, so the costs of organizing such a large group must be high" (2012, 45). Nevertheless, he argues that consumers have succeeded in organizing by developing a network style of campaigning that focuses broad coalitions on relatively specific issues. Networking is a form of "political 'hitchhiking,' enabling groups to hook up with particular causes and move faster than they would have been able to do on their own" (Hilton 2009, 149).

Many issues related to state protection take the form of entrepreneurial politics, where policies benefit a diffuse population but harm a concentrated one (Wilson 1980). Public health policy making, for instance, has been described as a classic case of entrepreneurial politics (Oliver 2006). In this situation, "policy entrepreneurs" become critical for mobilizing support and to do so they must often develop broad-based appeals (Kingdon 1984; Mintrom and Norman 2009). In Sweden, for example, policy entrepreneurs have been found to be prominent in health promotion issues related to children at the municipal level (Guldbrandsson and Fossum 2009); in the US state of Colorado, policy entrepreneurs have been found to be important in shaping the revision of the state's domestic violence treatment standards (Tunstall et al. 2016).

The precise character of advocacy depends on the policy sector. Occupational health and safety legislation in the UK has largely been achieved through corporatist deals between labor unions and employers with little involvement of the public (Demeritt et al. 2015), and union lobbying drove an expansion of similar legislation in the United States in the late 1960s (Ascher 2014). Child protection expanded in both the UK and the United States through the development of coalitions led by medical professions, but with growing public concern (Parton 1979; Myers 2008). In the food safety sector, coalition dynamics have been more complex on both sides of the Atlantic, involving many interests and professions working at different points in the food supply chain, often with substantial engagement by the general public (Demeritt et al. 2015; Swinnen 2015).

Historically, state protection often depends on how women's groups, consumers, and the labor movement interact to demand specific types of protections (Jensen 1989). While certain interests may take the lead in driving protective policies, they must often build broader coalitions to achieve success. For example, American unions were unable to displace a pro-market discourse about occupational health and safety until they framed the issue in a way that attracted a broader coalition (Shapiro 2014).

Coalitions may be quite broad. The coalition that passed the legislation creating the US Consumer Protection Financial Bureau after the 2008 financial crisis encompassed 250 consumer, housing, and labor groups (Kastner 2017). A European counterpart – Europeans for Financial Reform – created a similar coalition of several hundred groups. Ad hoc issue coalitions like these are prominent in both the EU and the United States, though there is more coalition activity in the United States (Mahoney 2007).

To mobilize support for a particular issue, advocacy groups often try to link up issues, such as obesity and health care costs (Kersh and Morone 2005; McBeth et al. 2013) or animal protection and genetically modified foods (Evans 2010). Alliances that cross partisan or class divides may also be important (Mares 2003), and the opportunity to create them may be increased by the weakening of party control over issues. In Denmark, for instance, political parties kept tobacco control off the political agenda, since no party had a strong incentive to campaign on the issue; weaker party cohesion permits cross-party coalitions and allows individual politicians to campaign on protective state issues (Albæk, Green-Pedersen, and Nielsen 2007).

Like the proverbial "Baptists and Bootleggers," protective state coalitions are often "strange bedfellow" coalitions (Vogel 2009). Human trafficking legislation in the United States grew out of a coalition of religious conservatives and feminists (Weitzer 2007), while recent flood insurance legislation was pushed through by a coalition of conservatives and environmentalists (Lehrer 2012). "Battered women" policies grew, in part, through an alliance of police, prosecutors, and battered women's advocates (Sack 2004), and disability policy was created by a "highly diverse reform coalition" (Melnick 1995, 26).

Protective state advocacy also mobilizes across local, national, and international levels. Such multilevel advocacy may take the form of advocacy groups strategically operating at different levels, as in the cases of Canadian pesticide politics (Pralle 2006) or European GMO debates (Ansell, Maxwell, and Sicurelli 2006). Multilevel networks may allow local and national groups to pool their resources to achieve global influence, as they have in consumer protection (Hilton 2009). The strategic framing of issues provides a basis for building these broad coalitions, as it did when the international community converged on criminalization as a frame for human trafficking in the 1990s and 2000s (Charnysh, Lloyd, and Simmons 2015).

Advocacy may also build around existing policies, programs, and institutions operating at different levels. The expansion of tobacco control in the United States developed through an interaction between the National Cancer Institute and local anti-smoking campaigns (Studlar 2014), while a similar multilevel alliance between the World Health Organization and the EU Commission's Directorate General for Health and Safety expanded tobacco control in Europe (Mamudu and Studlar 2009). Multilevel dynamics tend to empower advocacy coalitions that challenge the status quo (Princen 2007), as they have for obesity (Kurzer and Cooper 2011), alcohol (Butler et al. 2017), and toxic chemicals (Ansell and Balsiger 2011). However, multilevel dynamics may also multiply opportunities to veto policy change (Walti 2004).

3.2 Focusing Events and the Media

The politics of the protective state are often driven by events that dramatize the lack of state protection or the failure of state protection – the death of a child due to child abuse, a catastrophic natural disaster, or a medicine with shocking side effects (Carpenter and Sin 2007). Tragic focusing events can shift the "common sense causality" about what produces tragedies (McEvoy 1995). Such events are often critical for mobilizing diffuse publics to demand greater or more effective state protection (Birkland 1997). When interests are diffuse, a crisis can increase political salience and facilitate broad coalition building to produce protective state responses – as it did in the 2008 financial crisis (Kastner 2017). Focusing events rivet the attention of the media, the public, and politicians on problems and affect how public problems come to be framed (Lodge and Hood 2002; Fleming et al. 2016).

Focusing events can be either natural or human-made. Major floods, unsurprisingly, have been major factors in producing expansion of the state's role in flood policy (Johnson, Tunstall, and Penning-Rowsell 2005; Albright 2011; Knowles 2012; Roberts 2013; Bubeck et al. 2017; O'Donovan 2017). In England and Wales, major floods have increased the salience of reform ideas under consideration prior to a flood (Johnson, Tunstall, and Penning-Rowsell 2005). Moreover, as flooding has increasingly been understood as a foreseeable risk rather than an "act of God," media coverage of flooding in the UK has focused more on attributing blame (Escobar and Demeritt 2014). Although the distinction between "natural" and "human-made" hazards may be breaking down, some research finds that human-made focusing events may garner more attention and have a greater effect on the political agenda than natural hazards (Alexandrova 2015).

Focusing events are powerful, in part, because they galvanize attention to a public problem, often through elevated media coverage of an issue. In a study of how media reporting of a New York State bridge collapse led to national attention to the problem of bridge safety, Stallings (1990) points to two features of these media accounts that led to wider attention: first, successful accounts tend to identify the dramatic (but single) event as part of a pattern encompassing other similar events; second, successful accounts usually propose a causal explanation of this pattern that satisfactorily subsumes all known cases to date. Media attention can also raise the salience of risk (Kasperson and Kasperson 1996; Frewer, Miles, and Marsh 2002; Vasterman, Yzermans, and Dirkzwager 2005; Wardman and Löfstedt 2018), as it did, for instance, in the 2016 coverage of the Zika virus (Sell et al. 2018).

Media coverage may also contribute to a "culture of fear" (Glassner 1999; Wuthnow 2010). For example, Huffman (2016) argues that media attention to child murder cases in the 1990s reinforced fear among families and the public and created pressure for more stringent sex offender laws. However, the problem may not be sensationalism. Comparing news of the 1918 pandemic with more recent concern about pandemics, the sociologist Robert Wuthnow (2010) suggests that a key difference is the speed with which much wider publics become aware of the issues: "It is no accident that on any given day an informed person can hear about five ways in which the world might come crashing to an end" (2010, loc. 4963). Most contemporary threats are "distal" (not proximate), which means that we learn about them by "hearsay or general knowledge" (2010, loc. 4971).

Elevated issue attention can help to place issues on the agenda of political parties and legislatures and speed the production of responsive legislation (Wolfe 2012). However, scholars have found that the agenda-setting power of focusing events is quite varied. Reforms stemming from a focusing event may be vetoed by powerful political parties or institutions (Jensen 2011) or a cohesive status quo coalition (Hurka and Nebel 2013) or the interests of local communities (Bishop 2014). The ability of focusing events to produce policy change may depend on how they interact with wider political change (Albright 2011). In addition, focusing events may not produce new legislation or programs, but simply create pressure for quicker implementation of existing programs (Birkland and Lawrence 2009).

Public attention is often cyclical, and the result is that the politics of the protective state may operate like a "pendulum" swinging from stronger to weaker protection and back; this often looks like a swing between what Wilson (1980) calls "client politics" (dominated by interest groups facing concentrated costs or benefits) and "entrepreneurial politics" (where more diffuse public interests are episodically mobilized by entrepreneurs against "special interests"). Broad-based advocacy coalitions, scientific support, and sympathetic media attention galvanized by a regulatory/policy failure or some other focusing event are often necessary to mobilize this entrepreneurial politics.

Focusing events often create political opportunities for advancing certain agendas, in part by attributing blame (Kingdon 1984; Cobb and Primo 2003; Boin, 't Hart, and McConnell 2009; Lindholm 2017). Food safety scares may lead to criticism of government's capacity to govern "unruly markets" (Dunn 2007). A crisis, government failure, or a scandal can create public outrage and elevate a staid policy area to one of intense "noisy politics," "contested governance," or "forced choice" (Kitzinger 1999; Lodge and Hood 2002; Ansell and Vogel 2006; Kastner 2017). Crisis events often lead to reform of state institutions, though post-reform politics may also lead to "reversion to the mean" (Lodge and Hood 2002; Lodge 2011; Lægreid and Rykkja 2019).

3.3 Executive and Agency-Centered Political Mobilization

The politics of the protective state are often centered on the executive branch of government, which is expected to provide a rapid and authoritative protective response to actual and potential harms and threats. In the United States, the response to natural disasters has become "presidentialized" (Roberts 2013). The securitization of protective issues (like terrorism) also tends to accentuate executive powers and may provide justification for the exercise of these powers (Béland 2005).

The historical arc of the protective state has been to gradually develop specialized and expert public agencies to administer protective obligations. In the United States, public agencies like the Federal Aviation Administration, the Occupational Health and Safety Administration, or the Food and Drug Administration have been established to ensure the reliability of public protection (Adler 1995; O'Neil and Krane 2012; Carpenter 2014). Over time, and often in response to specific focusing events, such agencies have developed elaborate institutional arrangements for administering protective legislation. In the UK, the Health and Safety at Work Act 1974 "fundamentally transformed the institutional structure and legal principles for OHS regulation [and] consolidated the various specialist inspectorates within a new powerful regulatory agency, the Health and Safety Executive (HSE)" (Demeritt et al. 2015, 377). This consolidated agency increased the profile of occupational health and encouraged a more systemic approach to health and safety (Esbester and Almond 2017, 27).

Agencies institutionalize protective missions that have a basis in legal statutes. To fulfil these missions, agencies also develop skills, expertise, and techniques that allow them – indeed, require them – to detect and respond to threats. Wuthnow argues that expert agencies like the Atomic Energy Commission or the US Centers for Disease Control and Prevention (CDC) develop missions that require them to publicize fears (2010, loc. 3421). It is their job, he says, to anticipate worst-case scenarios and to conduct the monitoring and collect the information that enables them to evaluate the situation.

Agencies may also ally with advocacy groups to advance the state's protective capabilities (Carpenter 2001). Consumer protections in some countries (United States, UK, France) have developed via state-activist coalitions where advocacy groups and regulators expand protections to consumers (Trumbull 2012). Government departments that have a mission of promoting gender equality, for example, have helped to spearhead more comprehensive "violence against women" protection policies, often in cooperation with women's movements (Htun and Weldon 2012; Weldon and Htun 2013). In Sweden, child protection expanded beginning in the 1970s through a close relationship between child advocacy groups and the state (Lundström 2001). These "inside-outside" coalitions may be particularly important for representing diffuse interests (Kastner 2017).

While agencies are sometimes charged with having an interest in emphasizing threats to expand their jurisdictions or to consolidate their budgets, they are also accused of ignoring threats. Lead paint used in US public housing became a "hot potato" for national agencies that avoided responsibility for the issue, tragically delaying a response (Rosner and Markowitz 2016). In other cases, protective state issues have spilled over the sectoral boundaries of agencies and policy subsystems, as the issue of terrorism did after 2001 (Jochim and May 2010). These spillovers encourage "whole of government" strategies of protection – that is, strategies that mobilize government response across policy and agency boundaries (Christensen and Lægreid 2007; Trein 2017).

3.4 Science, Experts, and Politics

Science and the politics of science play a large role in building support for the protective state. Often the backing of science is important for convincing the public and politicians that protections are warranted. However, in many cases, the supporting science appears to be a necessary but not sufficient condition for protection. For example, the scientific and medical evidence of harm in the case of radon and asbestos was necessary but not sufficient to produce political support for protective policies in the United States (Scheberle 1994).

The boundaries between science, advocacy, and policy making are often blurred (Ezrahi 1990; Jasanoff 1990, 2011; Weingart 1999; Keller 2009). In some cases, advocacy groups may become critical sources of expertise, particularly when industry and government sources of expertise are distrusted (Ansell, Maxwell, and Sicurelli 2006; Loftstedt 2011; Cordner, Mulcahy, and Brown 2013; Kastner 2017). In other cases, experts and scientists may themselves act as advocacy groups (Lubitow 2013). For example, pediatricians drove the emergence of "child abuse" as a contemporary social problem (Pfohl 1977; Parton 1979), and public health experts have galvanized state action on obesity (Oliver 2005). In the area of infectious diseases, a group of prominent scientists has been critical in reawakening attention to the threats of global pandemics (Abraham 2011).

One way that scientists and experts influence protective state issues is through the medicalization of issues, whereby problems come to be defined in medical terms (Conrad 2007). Kersh and Morone (2002) argue that the medicalization of an issue is often a necessary step in the process of justifying more significant government action, especially when social movements and interest groups take it up. The production of statistics is another way that scientists and experts influence agenda setting on protective issues (Kingdon 1984). Statistics often amplify demands for protection but also can be used to dampen them – as they did in the case of traffic accident statistics (Vardi 2014).

3.5 The Entrepreneurial Politics of the Protective State

The best label to describe the politics of protection might be what political scientist James Q. Wilson's (1980) calls "entrepreneurial politics." Wilson argues that entrepreneurial politics occur when the benefits of state action are diffuse but the costs imposed are concentrated. Not all protective issues, of course, fit this description. Some protective state issues are better described as what Wilson calls "interest group politics," or "client politics," or "majoritarian politics." But many public health, consumer protection, environmental protection, and public security issues do promise diffuse public benefits while levying more concentrated costs.

The implication is that to get protective issues on the political agenda, advocacy groups and policy entrepreneurs typically need to build broad-based or multi-constituency coalitions and mobilize or leverage public attention. To do this, they must frame issues in ways that attract public attention and support demands for state protection. Events that galvanize the public's attention (focusing events) and mutually reinforcing actions between advocacy groups, the media, and science, however, are often necessary to tip the balance in favor of state protection. While the entrepreneurial politics of the protective state can be observed in all developed democratic nations, cross-national variations in political institutions can produce different varieties of the protective state – a topic to which we now turn.

4 Varieties of the Protective State

All developed countries have a protective state. However, just as compara-tive scholars have identified the "Three Worlds of Welfare Capitalism" or "Varieties of Capitalism," this section explores how the character and political dynamics of protective states differ cross-nationally. In some countries, constitutional provisions or legal systems grant greater protec-tions or facilitate the mobilization of protective rights. Welfare state tradi-tions also shape how issues are taken up by the protective state, with liberal welfare states often adopting a more regulatory and crisis-driven mode of protection. National modes of political negotiation also matter, with more pluralist and adversarial nations creating a more open political agenda for protective issues than corporatist and consensual nations. Nations with "consumerist" political and legal orientations also produce a more directly protectionist style than more "producerist" economies.

Although these institutional differences do produce different varieties of the protective state, it is not easy to array them along a single dimension of weak versus strong protective states. Rather, a nation may be strong on constitutional protections but also have a more restricted political agenda for protective issues.

4.1 State Traditions and the Constitutional and Legal Bases of Protection

States differ in their constitutional and legal obligations to protect citizens. Although the United States has greatly expanded the range of legal rights that provide protections (Epp 1998, 2010), the US Constitution does not clearly establish the national state's obligation to protect. In a landmark 1989 US Supreme Court decision, the Court ruled that the state does not have a legal obligation to protect the public from private harms unless it created those harms (Reich 2008; Dove 2013; Attanasio 2015; Beerman 2015; cf. Heyman 1991). Legal debates over this decision hinge on whether the Fourteenth Amendment creates a positive obligation to protect or simply a negative obligation not to harm.

By contrast, the German constitution explicitly defines the German state as a protective state (Rothstein, Boraz, and Huber, 2013). Historically, the German state's positive "duty of protection" (*Schutzpflicht*) originated in attempts to extend state protection to "unborn children," but this positive obligation was eventually applied across policy domains (Starck 2000; Huber 2008). Today, the stress on the state's positive obligation to protect the German people is manifest in policy areas as diverse as biosecurity and flooding (Lentzos and Rose 2009; Krieger 2013).

This constitutional obligation to protect interacts with Germany's "juridified" public administration to produce strong, but somewhat inflexible protections (Rothstein, Borraz, and Huber 2013). In contrast with German flood management, for instance, flood managers in the UK are freer of judicial constraints and thus have readily adopted flexible risk-based strategies of flood regulation (Krieger 2013). Even within a single country, however, legal constraints may vary by policy sector. In the UK, these more flexible risk-based strategies are used in the fields of flood management and occupational health and safety, but not in the area of food safety regulation where the state has an "absolute legal duty" to ensure that all food must be safe (Demeritt et al. 2015).

Over and above specific constitutional and legal constraints, state traditions are often important in explaining different approaches to protection (Christensen and Lodge 2018). When it comes to disasters, Sweden has a tradition of "comprehensive state protections"; recent challenges have reinforced this "total protection" approach (Amin 2013, 147, 150). Similarly, the French state has a "culturally established commitment" to provide security for French citizens that has "left no room for compromise with other objectives, such as employment or economic development" (Rothstein et al. 2013, 222, 223). As in Germany, this commitment works against the application of more flexible risk-based protection strategies.

In the domain of public health, France has also been more sensitive to "threats to the state" posed by disease than has the United States, which has been more sensitive to threats to individuals (Nathanson 2007a, 234). As a result, the French state invests in "reactive crisis management to maintain or restore public order and maintain the reputation of ministries" (Rothstein et al. 2013, 224). This strategy places stress on the development of early warning systems and contingency planning. The importance of this state tradition can be seen in France's response to biosecurity threats, which emphasizes contingency planning to anticipate even low-probability events (Lentzos and Rose 2009).

Although state traditions matter, statism is not a single dimension. Germany is typically regarded as more "statist" than "liberal" Britain, but it is also less statist in the sense that it often delivers social protections via intermediaries rather than by state agencies (Leisering and Mabbett 2011). Although German regulation is extensive, its corporatist approach to regulation tends to rely heavily on self-regulation. While constitutions or state traditions may provide a strong positive state obligation to protect citizens, this does not necessarily mean that the state is always open to new demands for protection. Neither Germany nor France was receptive to the demands of consumer groups or permitted the broad access to the courts granted in the United States (Trumbull 2006, 2012).

4.2 Regulatory Style, Science, and Risk Orientations

Different regulatory styles and orientations to science and to risk can also produce differences in how states extend protection (Adam, Hurka, and Knill 2017). Regulatory policy styles differ across Europe and between Europe and the United States. One frequently drawn distinction is between a largely American style of regulation that is more formal and adversarial versus a more cooperative style – prevalent in Europe, Canada, and Japan – that is less transparent and formal but also less conflictual (Kelman 1981; Vogel 1986; Harrison 1995; Kagan 2000, 2009; Wiktorowicz 2003).

The role of science in policy making also varies across countries. A study of how Germany, the UK, and the United States approached the debate about genetically modified organisms (GMOs) found that they embraced different "civic epistemologies" for handling risk (Jasanoff 2011). As noted earlier, the United States was found to be more adversarial than Germany or the UK. Although appeals to an autonomous or disinterested scientific community were important and frequent, science also tended to become quickly politicized. By contrast, Germany and the UK were more trusting of political elites. Germany, however, tended to rely on bureaucratic and corporatist strategies and public consultation to handle the GMO controversy, while the UK tended to place its faith in individual experts who achieved authority based on their reputation, experience, and public service.

Similar cross-national differences have also been observed in the field of public health (Nathanson 2007b). In countries like France or the UK, the authority of the regime and the authority of experts are strongly interdependent and can be reinforcing. Different points of view are incorporated directly into official government channels. In the French state, outcomes depend in part upon the relative prestige of different groups of technocratic elites. In the UK, the provision of official expertise is a "craft activity" of the "great and the good" who are called to serve by the state (Nathanson 2007b, 62–63). In both cases, risk controversies may be muted by the incorporation of science deliberation into the state. By contrast, as politics becomes more pluralistic – as it does in the

United States – knowledge claims become more competitive and politicized. In this world, the independence of science and scientists is highly valued but also less trusted.

Contrasts have also been drawn between "science-based" and "precautionary" or "value-based" regulatory cultures (Nestle 2003). In a science-based regulatory culture, decision making is narrowed to questions about scientific assessment of acceptable risk and focused on a specific accounting of the costs and benefits of the risk. By contrast, the precautionary or value-based approach adopts a wider perspective that emphasizes catastrophic or low-probability events and is concerned with public anxiety about risks.

A similar distinction is drawn between "risk-based" and "hazard-based" regulation. The former aims to assess the trade-offs between risks and benefits, while the later tends to adopt more outright bans on potential hazards (Lofstedt 2011). Although national and regional differences are not static, European nations and the EU are generally regarded as more precautionary/hazard/value-based than the United States (Vogel 2012). However, the differences are not necessarily always clear-cut (Wiener and Rogers 2002; Hammit et al., 2013). Sometimes the most salient differences are between different regulatory agencies rather than between nations (Lofstedt 2011).

Cross-national differences in how states manage protection may also be related to the dynamics of trust, transparency, and accountability. In countries with higher citizen trust in the state, such as Sweden or Denmark, more cooperative but less transparent regulatory arrangements are possible. However, in what Lofstedt (2011) calls "post-trust society," strong pressures can develop for transparency and accountability, and "risk-based" regulation may be one strategy of providing it (Rothstein, Borraz, and Huber 2013). As a protective strategy, the punitiveness of criminal justice systems may also be related to the trust in the state, with high-trust cultures like Norway more resistant to a culture of punitiveness than lower-trust cultures like the UK and the United States (Green 1997).

4.3 The Welfare State and Public Health

The traditional distinction between "universalist" and "residualist" welfare states has some important implications for understanding the different logics and consequences of protection (Esping-Andersen 2013). These implications extend beyond the welfare state, narrowly understood, to affect the regulatory state. In a universalist welfare state, like Sweden, the state provides comprehensive social protection. These comprehensive social protections may ameliorate public perceptions of risk because fundamental life risks are often dealt with by existing welfare programs. In a residualist welfare state like the United

States, however, the state tends to provide protection only as a last resort, and regulatory or punitive measures may take the place of service provision. Moreover, the limited social protection of residual welfare states may enhance public anxiety and lead to more politicized debate.

A comparison of how teenage pregnancy is dealt with in Sweden and the United States illustrates this contrast. In Sweden, teenage pregnancy has not been a particularly prominent public issue. Instead, the issue has been absorbed into the institutions of the welfare state, which provide comprehensive health and welfare services. Teenage mothers are accommodated within this universalist welfare state arrangement. In the United States, by contrast, support for teen mothers is limited, and the welfare state is criticized for contributing to the problem. The issue has been highly visible and marked by contentious moralistic debate, with limited agreement about how to remedy the problem (Linders and Bogard 2014).

The issue of child abuse also offers a lens into the different strategies of protection. In social democratic welfare states, protection of children from family abuse is embedded in a wider system of providing general welfare services to families. In more liberal (e.g., residualist) welfare states, child protection is more likely to be provided as a stand-alone regulatory function via "child protection" agencies. In the latter context, social services for families are limited and the protective role becomes more legalized and punitive. Although some convergence may be occurring in child welfare models, these differences continue to be salient (Gilbert 2012; on variations within the United States, see Edwards 2016).

These differences in approaches to child welfare shape, in turn, the political dynamics of the child abuse issue. In countries with a more regulatory approach, such as in Anglo-American democracies, the issue of child protection has been characterized by a poisonous political dynamic that links scandalous child deaths, public outrage, and perpetual reform demands (Ayre 2001; Douglas 2009; Gainsborough 2009; Chenot 2011; Jagannathan and Camasso 2011; Mansell, Erasmus, and Marks 2011). Where welfare states are weaker, the victimization of children becomes the ultimate weapon for demanding protection; they are the ultimate victims who cannot be held responsible for risks and harms.

Nations with liberal (in the European rather than the American sense) welfare systems may also be more prone to moral panics and the politics of victimization. For example, although policies toward sex offenders have become more punitive in many countries, Anglo-American democracies appear to be particularly prone to moral panics and victimization on this issue (Petrunik and Deutschmann 2008). Wacquant (2009) argues that the neoliberal shift from welfare to work has increased anxieties about marginal populations, leading the state to adopt a more punitive approach to these populations.

The character of national welfare states may also shape the kinds of issues that rise up on the agenda of protective states. For example, the stronger focus on children's environmental health in the United States than in Canada arises because the greater national attention to health care in Canada trumps the narrower focus on children's environmental health (Boothe and Harrison 2009). A recurring theme here is that the weak or submerged welfare state in the United States in some ways redirects concerns toward protection of certain "victims" or "rights" against specific risks. As welfare states become more universalistic, social protections target broader publics.

Public health also varies in strength and character cross-nationally, affecting the protective role of the state. Differences in the relationship of health professions to the state are one important factor (Trein 2017). Where professions are strong and develop independently of the state – as they have in Australia, the UK, and the United States – professionals must also take public positions that often place them in an advocacy role. By contrast, where professionalism is weaker and dominated by the state – as in Germany and Switzerland – the demands of public health professionals are accommodated through established corporatist relations, and they have less incentive to engage in independent political activity. In the case of tobacco control, the German medical profession did not take the lead in promoting anti-smoking, as the profession did in other countries (Grüning, Strünck, and Gilmore 2008).

A key factor in the relative strength of public health is the relationship that develops between national health systems, clinical medicine, and public health (Trein 2018). It is difficult to draw any sharp boundary between public health and clinical medicine, but generally the former focuses on population health, while the later focuses on treating individuals. In universalist welfare states, population health and clinical medicine tend to be integrated into national health care systems, producing strong public health protections (Mackenbach and McKee 2013). However, in some cases, like France, the public health dimensions of national health care systems are much weaker than the clinical dimension (Nathanson 2007b).

States also vary in terms of the relative power of public health and clinical medicine. Duffy describes the US public health system as constrained by "the reluctance of public health officers to clash with the AMA [American Medical Association]" (Duffy 1992, 294). Although clinical medicine and public health may be at odds, they may also reinforce each other in various ways. For example, if the costs of clinical care in national health care systems increase, nations may have strong incentives to invest in preventive public health care measures.

4.4 Political Institutions and Patterns of Interest Aggregation

Protective states reflect differences in how institutions shape the expression and aggregation of political interests. One institutional contrast that has merit in understanding differences in protective states is the classical contrast between majoritarian and proportional electoral systems, which affects how political interests are mobilized and aggregated (Lijphart 2012). Gunnar Trumbull (2012) argues that the representation of consumer interests depends on how political systems represent diffuse interests. He argues that the majoritarian electoral system and the liberal market economy in the United States tend to favor diffuse interests associated with consumers, while the proportional representation and corporatist institutions of Germany favor more "sectoral" interests like labor and employers.

The distinction between pluralist and corporatist forms of interest group bargaining is also important (Berger 1983). In more pluralist forms of mobilization, interest groups tend to be more fragmented and decentralized and engage with the state more through lobbying. Interest mobilization is often fluid and competitive with less organized political negotiation, which creates a more open political agenda. By contrast, corporatism is characterized by unified and centralized interest mobilization and more institutionalized patterns of political negotiation, creating a more cooperative but less open political style. Corporatism is generally thought to produce a cumulative and consensual policy style that dampens crisis-driven or alarmist policy making (Coleman, Skogstad, and Atkinson 1996).

Pluralist and corporatist interest group patterns may produce different protective state outcomes. In the area of occupational health and safety, pluralist union lobbying in the United States led to more of a state regulatory regime, while labor mobilization in Sweden led to the development of worker-management safety committees where workers had a majority (Ascher 2014). Strong corporatism in Scandinavia has also facilitated negotiation between employers and organized consumer groups that has resulted in strong consumer protection (Trumbull 2012). However, as noted, corporatism can also produce a less open policy process that keeps protective issues off the political agenda. In the case of tobacco control, corporatist policy making in Germany and Denmark has favored the tobacco industry over health considerations (Albæk, Green-Pedersen, and Nielsen 2007; Grüning, Strünck, and Gilmore 2008).

4.5 Producerism versus Consumerism

A related distinction is between producerism and consumerism. Again, the contrast distinguishes Continental European legal regimes from more liberal legal regimes. Continental European legal regimes are characterized as having a stronger producer orientation, because they have historically been less concerned about cartel arrangements and have extended strong legal protections to labor. By contrast, the US legal regime is characterized as more consumerist in orientation due to its strong anti-monopoly orientation and its less generous attitude toward labor protection (Whitman 2007). The United States has also been considered among the first consumer societies in the sense that it valorizes individual choice within a market society (Trentmann 2004). Although many aspects of consumerism have diffused from the United States to other nations, Continental Europe has tended to view consumers more in terms of social citizenship than in terms of their relationship to the functioning of the market (De Grazia 2009).

Both producerism and consumerism are compatible with consumer protection in the sense of protecting consumers from the ills of the market. However, there are differences in the logic of how protection is extended to consumers. In Continental Europe, consumers are not defined as having an economic interest per se. Rather, they are understood as citizens who require state protection from problems caused by markets. American-style consumerism, by contrast, understands consumers as sovereign economic actors. US consumer protection has often been established by creating a "private right of action" – a right that allows consumers to use the courts to redress individual or class action harms (Schwartz and Silverman 2005).

In the United States, rights-based consumer mobilization has been partly linked to and modeled on the civil rights movement (Hilton 2009; Kastner 2017), while European consumers have tended to ally with the labor movement (Trumbull 2006, 2012). To some extent, patterns of consumer protection have partially converged. For example, Trumbull finds that both the United States and France have developed a rights-based protection model even though this model grew out of different background assumptions and institutions. In France, consumers were regarded as vulnerable and in need of state protection while the US model grew out of a combination of political and judicial activism (Strünck 2015).

Differences within Europe are also important. Both Germany and Sweden have strong corporatist patterns that have shaped consumer outcomes. However, in Germany (and Japan and Austria), consumer protection has been marked by strong industry-state alliances, leading to a cooperative regulatory regime that emphasizes the importance of providing consumers with information. By contrast, in Sweden (and Denmark and Norway), consumer protection has been marked by a strong industry-consumer activist alliance that allows consumer movements to bargain with industry and the state (Hilton 2009;

Trumbull 2012). Despite these differences, Denmark, France, Germany, Sweden, and the UK all enjoy high public confidence in national consumer protection (Brasoveanu, Brasoveanu, and Mascu 2014).

Finally, countries differ in terms of the political organization and mobilization of consumers. In Scandinavia and the United States, consumer mobilization has been relatively strong, while in Germany it has been more limited (Trumbull 2012). An interesting feature of consumer activism is that it is often supported by women and thus interacts with women's mobilization (Hilton 2009, 56–57, 60). In the United States, consumerism has historically expanded opportunities for women to mobilize politically (Cohen 2003); in Denmark, the Danish housewives' associations (*De Danske Husmoderforeninger*) were the kernel of an expanding consumer movement (Trumbull 2012).

4.6 Summary

The differences in protective states are complex, and this section has only drawn out some very general patterns. Indeed, we should be cautious in attributing differences to national contrasts because sometimes the key variation is sectoral rather than cross-national. Moreover, there is often quite a bit of convergence in the policy styles of protective states. Nevertheless, this section suggests that some broad differences may be important. The most salient division appears to be between a more statist or corporatist politics, on the one hand, and a more liberal or pluralist politics, on the other.

This distinction is relatively standard in the literature on comparative public policy. What is more novel about the contrast is how it suggests particular styles of protective state politics, particularly in liberal and pluralist countries like the United States. In this case, a residualist welfare state provides limited social protections, which leads in turn to a greater use of regulatory and punitive instruments to achieve protections for narrower categories of actors (e.g., "child protection"). Private rights are mobilized to both limit and expand claims for state protection, and pluralist interest group mobilization creates an open political agenda for advancing new protective demands. Science is appealed to as a neutral arbiter of risk decisions, and scientists and experts retain greater autonomy from the state than in statist and corporatist nations. But the flip side of this autonomy is a greater politicization of science.

In liberal and pluralist settings, the limited basis of the state's obligations to protect, the narrower targets of protective politics, and the more adversarial character of politics tend to interact to produce more piecemeal and politicized protective policies. Moreover, the protective politics of liberal and pluralist nations tend to be more crisis-driven, moralistic, and distrustful and more likely to be driven by a politics of fear and victimization than in statist or corporatist settings. In part, this may be because strong emotive justifications are needed to mobilize support for state protection.

Although a crisis-driven politics of fear and victimization can be detected in statist and corporatist countries too, it occurs in a dampened form. Science is politicized to some degree everywhere, and the rough-and-tumble of interest group politics is certainly not limited to liberal and pluralist countries. Yet, in ideal-typical terms, this contrast does suggest an important difference in the character of protective state politics.

5 Political Theory and the Protective State

The protective state claims to protect citizens against bad things happening – harms, accidents, hazards, threats, and risks. This claim lies at the heart of an implicit social contract between the state and its citizens – implicit because it is often expressed only when the state "fails" to protect or when it is seen as overreaching its protective role. In the face of tragedies like the mad cow scandal, the Tōhoku tsunami, or the Flint water crisis, advocacy groups and the public demand that the state be held accountable for its failure to protect. Yet as controversies over security surveillance, the soda tax, or "stop and frisk" policies suggest, the protective state may also be criticized for going too far. The frontiers of this social contract are fluid and disputed and ultimately depend on politics.

The state's obligation to protect is a matter of dispute in moral, legal, and political theory (Attanasio 2015). Perhaps the classic statement of how to balance the obligations and limitations of the state's protective role was advanced by the nineteenth-century liberal political philosopher John Stuart Mill. His "harm principle" argues that the state should only intervene to limit the freedom of citizens to prevent harm to other citizens. More recently voiced arguments have critiqued or defended the protective role of the state on quite different philosophical grounds. French sociologist Michel Foucault's critique of the liberal "surveillance state" and German political theorist Carl Schmitt's positive defense of the state's exceptional use of emergency powers are two notable examples.

This final section turns to a wider discussion of the political theory of the protective state. A political theory of the state, in general, is concerned with the interpretation and justification of state power. To protect, the state must intervene, often using coercive and regulatory powers to protect some individuals and groups from others, or even from themselves.

5.1 Classical Liberalism

The rich philosophical and political tradition of classical liberalism has a Janus-faced view of protection. On the one hand, the liberal political tradition regards protection as "not only government's first duty; it is government's first purpose" (Dove 2013, 63; see also Heyman 1991–92). The social contract between state and society obliges the state to protect citizens. On the other hand, classical liberalism has an equal regard for the need to protect citizen *from* the state. The criminologist David Garland expresses this dual role well when he writes of "liberalism's twin concern to maximize freedom of action and to reduce that freedom's harmful consequences" (2003, 64). The liberal tradition discusses this twin concern in terms of the need to find a balance between liberty and security (Waldron 2006) – a balance, it is worth noting, that can shift dramatically over time. Writing of the 1970s through 1990s, Garland observes that "[t]he call for protection *from* the state has been increasingly displaced by the demand for protection *by* the state" (2001, 12; emphasis in original).

The liberal tradition is concerned with the issue of where the state can legitimately intervene to constrain the autonomy of individual citizens. As noted, John Stuart Mill's harm principle is perhaps the most important liberal statement of this concern. Mill expresses this principle as follows: "the only purpose for which power can be rightfully exercised over any member of a civilised community, against his will, is to prevent harm to others" (Mill 1865, 6). This principle suggests that individual autonomy should be respected unless an individual's actions potentially harm others. The harm principle is powerful because it offers a standard for balancing liberalism's twin concern of protection by and from the state.

Classical liberalism is not, of course, the only political theory to evaluate the obligations and limits of state protection. Classical or "civic" republicanism has a somewhat different take on freedom, associating freedom with non-domination rather than with noninterference or non-coercion. To illustrate the difference, the political philosopher Philip Pettit argues that classical republicanism stresses the importance of "free people" in contrast with liberalism's emphasis on "free choice" (2015, 1058). This emphasis on "free people" leads to a different standard for when the state can and should intervene to provide protection. Although classical republicanism has no concise analogy to the harm principle, it suggests that the state can intervene to prevent domination and to encourage active and equal citizenship. For example, it might support "a moral vision of freeing a population of individuals from the burden of disease in order that they may lead more productive and happier lives" (Jennings 2007, 43).[5]

---

[5] For a reinterpretation of the harm principle in ways consistent with the republican principle of non-domination, see Ripstein (2006). Ripstein's interpretation, however, strikes me as a narrower than the one suggested by Pettit (2015). For a critique of the argument that liberalism and republicanism have sharply different perspectives on public health intervention, see Nielsen (2011).

A "social democratic" position on protection can also be discerned. From this perspective, "a general reduction of risk and insecurity" is necessary for a free and egalitarian citizenship (Marshall and Bottomore 1992, 38). The state is responsible for promoting the "equal dignity" of citizens (Pettit 1987, 549). In contrast with the classical liberal position, a social democratic perspective begins by reasoning about the collective welfare of citizens rather than from the autonomy or liberty of individual citizens. A similar "public interest" perspective on protection emphasizes that protection is a democratically sanctioned social value (Shapiro and Glicksman 2003). For example, in a study of US occupational health and safety, legal scholar Sidney Shapiro writes that the commitment to the protection of workers that developed in the 1960s and 1970s expressed a "democratic goal – one rooted in understanding the protection of workers as a social objective, rather than as a backup for the failure of market transactions" (2014, 841).

Although important alternative perspectives exist, Mill's harm principle remains highly influential, particularly in legal reasoning. Moreover, its use has grown in a variety of ways to encompass discrimination, harms to nature, and harms that befall a person from natural causes (Epstein 1995), and it is being used politically where moral reasoning was once used (Harcourt 1999). For instance, pornography can be argued to be harmful to women rather than simply being immoral. Both sides in political disputes also increasingly invoke the harm principle. Opponents of drug liberalization can argue in favor of state regulation of drugs on the ground that it causes harm to drug users, while proponents can argue for drug liberalization by pointing to the harms caused by these laws to minority groups. The harm principle has become central to the legal, philosophical, and political debates about protection.

5.2 The Nanny State and the "Nudge"

Can the state protect you even when you do not want protection? Motorcycle helmet laws provide the archetypical example. Can we require people to wear helmets even if not wearing the helmet does not hurt others? Although public health advocates have provided epidemiological evidence that not wearing a helmet leads to fatalities, biker advocacy groups in a number of US states have successfully argued that wearing a helmet is a matter of personal choice (Jones and Bayer 2007). Following Mill's harm principle, regulation can only be justified if we can identify the harms that the biker imposes on others by not wearing a helmet. A possible argument for regulation is that others have to bear the medical costs of motorcycle accidents. Such was the story with expanding smoking regulation, which was advanced when people became convinced of the public medical costs of smoking and the health effects of secondhand smoke (Wood 2006).

Although demonstrating wider societal costs provides justification for state intervention under the harm principle, a more challenging philosophical question is whether the state can intervene to protect individuals against themselves. In legal terms, state intervention in such cases is called "paternalistic." Following from Mill's harm principle, legal philosopher Gerald Dworkin defines paternalism as "the interference with a person's liberty of action justified by reasons referring exclusively to the welfare, good, happiness, needs, interests, or values of the person being coerced" (1972, 65). Such interferences have led to a powerful negative framing of an overreaching state as the "nanny state," which treats adults like children, "not letting them do anything fun" (Wiley, Berman, and Blanke 2013, 90). The anti–nanny state position can be ironically summed up as follows: "Sure, people are worried about lung cancer and heart disease and diabetes. But who wants to give up cigarettes and caramel lattes and huge buckets of buttery popcorn in favor of tap water and broccoli and jogging?" (Wiley, Berman, and Blanke 2013, 88). State protection potentially violates the autonomy of individuals to make their own choices (Gostin and Gostin 2009).

Such interventions are sometimes justified in terms of preventing people from making bad or irrational choices (Friedman 2013). If people lack appropriate information or if they make bad choices due to addiction or coercion, interventions may be justified (again, from a classical liberal perspective). This position is sometimes called "soft paternalism," and the criterion for judging these interventions is whether the behavior of those to be protected is "substantially voluntary" (Pope 2003, 667–68). In other words, if the individual does not have the information, will, or capacity to make a reasonable choice, then state intervention may be warranted. To be clear, "soft" paternalism substitutes "regulatory judgment" for "personal judgment" (Friedman 2013, 1698).

Arguably, soft paternalism is not paternalism at all, because autonomy did not exist in the first place. Indeed, such an intervention might be construed as one that restores autonomy and rationality to people. However, soft paternalism does restrict liberty, since it intervenes to prohibit people from making what the state regards as bad choices. Therefore, under the liberal view of soft paternalism, the state may intervene to restore autonomy and rationality only if the intervention intends to protect an individual from a harm or leads to a benefit to the individual (the state's motivation for intervention cannot be strictly selfish).

In contrast to soft paternalism, "hard paternalism" occurs when the state intervenes to limit liberty for benevolent purposes even when people *do not lack* information, will, or capacity to act in a particular way (Pope 2003). Returning to the example of motorcycle helmet laws (and suspending any claim of negative spillover effects on health care costs), hard paternalism applies if the state forces motorcyclists to wear helmets even if they are well informed about the potential health dangers of not wearing a helmet. In hard paternalism, the state either disregards or intentionally limits a person's autonomous choice by imposing restrictions on liberty for benevolent purposes.

Another approach to the issue of paternalism is to focus on the nature of the state's intervention and the way that it constrains or restrains liberty. The most important statement of this perspective is what Sunstein and Thaler (2003) call "libertarian paternalism." Building on behavioral economics, they argue that governments can design information, rules, and institutions to encourage better choices. These designs should be "libertarian" in the sense that they should – in contrast with helmet laws – allow people to opt out. These interventions should be "liberty preserving," and they should "nudge" rather than force (Sunstein 2014). However, they are paternalistic in that they try to influence choices in particular ways even when negative spillovers on third parties are not present. To return to the example of smoking, a libertarian paternalistist would be comfortable with the state taking steps to discourage people from smoking even without appealing to the rationale of increased collective health costs or the health effects of secondhand smoke. The state could take these paternalistic steps as long as individuals are ultimately free to choose to smoke if they so desire.

The harm principle and this issue of paternalism offer one way to think about the protective state's limits and obligations. However, we reach different conclusions if we start with a more sociological view of risk.

5.3 Risk Society

As noted in Section 2, the most sweeping contemporary statement about risk is without a doubt Ulrich Beck's now classic statement on "risk society." His perspective is a powerful one because it places our current concerns about risk at the center of an analysis of fundamental societal change. His central thesis is that a change has been occurring that is as fundamental as the shift from feudal to modern society. "Modernization," writes Beck, "is becoming reflexive; it is becoming its own theme" (Beck 1992, 19). With this statement, Beck argues that there has been a major shift in societal perspective – from a relatively unreflexive valuing of technology and economic development as a way of improving our quality of life to an obsession with the risks produced by those same developments.

Beck's analysis of risk society is both sweeping and profound and, not surprisingly, it leads Beck to a distinctive political theory of contemporary society. He argues that the risk society decenters politics from its conventional political channels – e.g., parliament and political parties – into the previously less-politicized spheres of science, economy, and technology. A more active citizenry mobilized in fluid social movements is the agent of this politicization. The result, Beck writes, is somewhat paradoxical: *"political modernization disempowers and unbinds politics and politicizes society"* (1992, 194, emphasis in original). The positive way out of this paradoxical situation is a democratization of technology and economic development.

Beck's idea about democratizing risk, along with his emphasis on the incalculability of risks and their potentially catastrophic nature, dovetails with debates about the precautionary principle. The French historian and philosopher François Ewald argues that the precautionary principle is "one of the primary instruments of 'reflexive modernization'" (1999, 73). While debates about the precautionary principles are complex and extensive, it useful here to focus on a few points related to Beck's risk society perspective. From this point of view, the precautionary principle realizes the democratization of risk because it moves beyond a paradigm that asserts that science and experts are fully capable of making decisions and controlling risks; it widens the scope of public input into the decision-making process.

As a strategy of democratizing risk, one claim is that the precautionary principle shifts the burden of proof under conditions of uncertainty (Scott 2005). That is, those who undertake risky actions should have to demonstrate that their actions are not harmful. Another claim is that the precautionary principle demands wider deliberation about the intergenerational dimensions of risk management (Johnson 2007) and entails a requirement "for not only substantive, but also procedural and discursive rationality" (Kysar 2006, 10). Critics of the precautionary principle, however, point to how a precautionary approach ignores opportunity costs (Sunstein 2002, 2005).

Issues about the democratization of risk are often framed in terms of "expert" versus "populist" views of risk. Divergences between expert and public perceptions of risk have been extensively discussed (Schrader-Frechette 1991; Jasanoff 1998; Wynne 2001; Klinke and Renn 2002; Sunstein 2002b; Slovic et al. 2004). Such debates often lead to an exploration of how to expand the role of the public in risk decision making, often through various strategies of expanding "deliberative democracy" (Klinke and Renn 2002, 2018; Montpetit and Rouillard 2008).

Note the very different tenor of discussion here in contrast with the earlier discussion of classical liberalism and the harm principle. Beginning with a concern for balancing liberty and security, the liberal analysis becomes focused on a legal and ethical justification for when the state can intervene. However, beginning with the risk society thesis, we are led to a more precautionary attitude toward risk and to a concern with expanding the public's role in risk decision making. A third set of political theory perspectives on the protective state arises from debates about "neoliberalism."

5.4 Critiques of Neoliberalism

While Beck's risk society argument leads to a concern with the democratization of risk, another contemporary line of social critique raises an ominous note about the character of modern government. This critique focuses on neoliberalism, a prominent theme in discussions of the transformation of the state over the past couple of decades. Although there are many discussions of what "neoliberalism" means, it is used here to refer to the extension of the logic and discipline of markets, with their calculative and disciplinary rationality, into the political domain of the state and citizenship, such that both state institutions and state-society relationships are reconfigured (Ong 2006).

One argument about the neoliberal state is that it is punitive (Wacquant 2009, 2010). By scaling back the provision of welfare and constructing a "workfare" state, neoliberalism increases the social insecurity of its citizens. To address this social insecurity, the neoliberal state directs more punitive measures against the lower classes. The result is a major expansion of a prison state that mirrors the shrinking of traditional welfare supports. Thus, protection from crime becomes a major issue that supports the legitimacy of the neoliberal state. A key implication of this argument is that while neoliberalism advances the values of freedom and autonomy associated with a market society, it also reinforces the coercive arm of the state and elevates concern about security.

Work inspired by Michel Foucault's analysis of liberalism and the state has developed a different kind of critique of neoliberalism. For Foucault, neoliberalism arises as a search for political techniques to govern while restricting the expansion of the state (Rose, O'Malley, and Valverde 2006). This is done by promoting self-governing or what Foucault called "governmentality" and by encouraging individual subjects to internalize the calculative and disciplinary rationality of markets. In the Foucaultian tradition, this extension of market rationality to citizens is referred to as "responsibilization," which is understood to be a "technology of self-governing" (Ong 2006). As Foucault scholar Thomas Lemke summarizes: "Neo-liberalism is a political rationality that tries to render the social domain economic and to link a reduction in (welfare) state services and security systems to the increasing call for 'personal responsibility' and 'self-care'" (2001, 203).

Thus, neoliberal governmentality favors "governing at a distance" through the subjectivity of citizens. While reinforcing the autonomy of citizens, it stresses their need to behave in a prudential fashion and to take responsibility for their own fate. To refer back to our earlier discussion of libertarian paternalism, nudge strategies are sometimes seen as a prime example of neoliberal governmentality (Leggett 2014; Esmark 2018). Foucault's ideas have been used to interpret the shifting role of the state in providing (or limiting) protection. For example, it is argued that flood protections have evolved toward a strategy of neoliberal governmentality in the UK because they have tried to shift responsibility onto citizens (Butler and Pidgeon 2011).

Foucault's analysis has also led to a critique of the concept of "resilience," which has been increasingly used in recent years to talk about societal security. From a Foucaultian perspective, resilience represents a form of neoliberal governmentality and an embodiment of responsibilization. The language of resilience is seen to be part of a neoliberal discourse that places limits on the state's obligations to protect while encouraging individuals to take responsibility for their own protection (Chandler 2013; Coaffee 2013; Joseph 2013; Hutter, Leibenath, and Mattissek 2014; Tierney 2015). It is worth pointing out, however, that the term may have different meanings in different contexts. For example, in the UK, resilience does imply greater self-reliance, but in Sweden the term has been used to expand state protections (Lentzos and Rose 2009; Amin 2013).

A final issue that deserves mention here is the idea developed in the governmentality literature about the expansion of the "surveillance state," which builds on Foucault's description of prison control via the "panopticon" – an architectural style that allows for easy and comprehensive surveillance and control (Foucault 2012). Although classical liberal theory is also concerned about how surveillance can undermine freedom and privacy (Balkin 2008), a number of critical theorists have begun to call attention to how neoliberalism interacts with securitization, resilience, and surveillance to produce new technologies of social control (Coaffee and Fussey 2015). These critiques have led to heightened concerns about the state's expansion of surveillance in the age of terrorism.

5.5 Crisis, the State of Exception and Securitization

The work on neoliberal governmentality is not the only critical theory tradition advancing concern about the protective state. Another body of critical work focuses on the nature of security and draws on the work of Weimar political theorist Carl Schmitt's analysis of crisis and "the state of exception." As Schmitt famously writes, "Sovereign is he who decides on the exception" (Schmitt 1985 [1922], 5). While constitutions and legal rules can provide general norms to rule many situations, Schmitt argues that these norms are inapplicable during a crisis or emergency. The state of exception is outside of – ungoverned by – law. The conclusion is not only that crisis momentarily suspends law, revealing true power, but more disturbingly that the "state of exception" can be used to assert dictatorial powers that operate beyond the law. Agamben (2005) argues that the US Patriot Act, passed after the September 11 attack, provides a contemporary example of this state of exception because it suspended international law by ignoring the legal status of detainees.

To put this issue in terms of the protective state, one danger is that the state may use protection as an excuse to suspend law during crises and emergencies. French President François Holland's lengthy emergency declaration after the November 15, 2015, terrorist attack in Paris raised such concerns. A related but somewhat different concern is that exceptional politics (e.g., exemplified by post–September 11 politics) will institutionalize a politics of fear that may erode liberal democracy (Huysmans 2004; cf. Williams 2011). Some scholars, however, are dubious of the Schmittian perspective, pointing out that contemporary emergencies are not lawless (Auriel 2018).

Beyond the discussion of the state of exception, a critical literature also challenges expansive notions of security. Security – particularly the term "national security" – has traditionally been used with respect to the idea of protecting the territorial integrity of the nation and the state. Initiating a discussion that came to be known as the Copenhagen School of Security Studies, Ole Wæver argues that in the 1980s there was a "move from a strict focus on the security of the *state* (national security) toward a broader or alternative focus on the security of *people*" (1995, 47; emphasis in original). More generally, the Copenhagen School suggests that securitization is a political and discursive act that can be extended to many situations and issues.

While the Copenhagen school does not invariably see securitization as a negative feature of modern politics, it does express concern that securitization often breaks (unjustifiably) with normal politics – that it is a politics of "speed" and "silence" rather than "deliberation" and "debate" (Aradau 2004; Roe 2012, 251). Scholars have begun to link the idea of the state of exception to that of securitization, arguing that emergencies are analogous to wars. For example, Hanrieder and Kreuder-Sonnen (2014) argue for what they call "the emergency trap" – where a state of exception drives a further securitization of issues. They argue that the SARS epidemic in 2003 led to an expansion of the World Health Organization's emergency powers and a securitization of the issue of pandemic response.

Discussions about securitization have led to exploration of how the negative effects of securitization can be counteracted. International relations scholar Claudia Aradau (2004) argues that the negative effects of securitization should be counterbalanced by a politics of emancipation, one that democratically mobilizes concerns about equality and fairness. Another argument, advanced by Michael Williams (2011), is that a "liberalism of fear," or what he calls a "fear of fear," may offer a corrective restraint on the negative aspects of securitization. A similar argument by Vibeke Schou Tjalve (2011) suggests that the Atlantic tradition of Republicanism – with its concern for a vigorous public sphere – can serve as a check on securitization. All of these arguments, to one extent or another, call for a mobilization of democratization to counter the potentially illiberal aspects of securitization.

5.6 Concluding Thought

The central theme of this Element is that "protection" lies at the heart of what the modern democratic state is, what it does, and how it legitimates itself. The state protects its territory from attack and its citizens from disease and crime; it protects property, critical infrastructure, and the environment; it protects consumers, children, and animals. This protective role is so ubiquitous, and perhaps so natural, that it is oddly overlooked as a common crosscutting element of the modern state. We easily recognize that the state protects citizens from crime, the environment from degradation, or consumers from fraud. But there is limited recognition that protection is a powerful common theme across a wide range of policy sectors.

This final section has examined the political theory of the protective state. Both the state's obligations to protect and the limits of its interventions deserve greater attention. With its twin concern for liberty and security, the liberal tradition has paid the most sustained attention to this issue and offers the most concrete practical guidelines for ordering the state's protective role. Although contemporary critical theory traditions – from Ulrich Beck's risk society to Michel Foucault's perspective on neoliberal governmentality – have opened up new perspectives on the protective state, we are still in need of more political theory exploration of when, why, and how the state should protect its citizens from harms, risks, and threats – an issue that is not going away anytime soon.

References

Abraham, T. (2011). The chronicle of a disease foretold: Pandemic H1N1 and the construction of a global health security threat. *Political Studies*, 59(4), 797–812.

Adam, C., Hurka, S., & Knill, C. (2017). Four styles of regulation and their implications for comparative policy analysis. *Journal of Comparative Policy Analysis*, 19(4), 327–344.

Adler, R. S. (1995). Redesigning people versus redesigning products: The Consumer Product Safety Commission addresses misuse. *Journal of Law & Politics*, 11, 79–127.

Agamben, G. (2005). *State of Exception*, trans. Kevin Attell. Chicago: University of Chicago Press.

Albæk, E., Green-Pedersen, C., & Nielsen, L. B. (2007). Making tobacco consumption a political issue in the United States and Denmark: The dynamics of issue expansion in comparative perspective. *Journal of Comparative Policy Analysis*, 9(1), 1–20.

Albertson, B., & Gadarian, S. K. (2015). *Anxious Politics: Democratic Citizenship in a Threatening World*. Cambridge: Cambridge University Press.

Albright, E. A. (2011). Policy change and learning in response to extreme flood events in Hungary: An advocacy coalition approach. *Policy Studies Journal*, 39(3), 485–511.

Alexandrova, P. (2015). Upsetting the agenda: The clout of external focusing events in the European Council. *Journal of Public Policy*, 35(3), 505–530.

Allen, M. D. (2005). Laying down the law? Interest group influence on state adoption of animal cruelty felony laws. *Policy Studies Journal*, 33(3), 443–457.

Almond, P., & Esbester, M. (2018). Regulatory inspection and the changing legitimacy of health and safety. *Regulation & Governance*, 12(1), 46–63.

Amin, A. (2013). Surviving the turbulent future. *Environment and Planning D: Society and Space*, 31(1), 140–156.

Amoore, L. (2013). *The Politics of Possibility: Risk and Security beyond Probability*. Durham: Duke University Press.

Andreas, P., & Price, R. (2001). From war fighting to crime fighting: Transforming the American national security state. *International Studies Review*, 3(3), 31–52.

Ansell, C., & Balsiger, J. (2011). Circuits of regulation: Transatlantic perspectives on persistent organic pollutants and endocrine disrupting chemicals. In D. Vogel & J. F. Swinnen, eds., *Transatlantic Regulatory Cooperation: The Shifting Roles of the EU, the US and California*. Cheltenham: Edward Elgar Publishing, pp. 180–199.

Ansell, C., & Baur, P. (2018). Explaining trends in risk governance: How problem definitions underpin risk regimes. *Risk, Hazards & Crisis in Public Policy*, 9(4), 397–430.

Ansell, C., Maxwell, R., & Sicurelli, D. (2006). Protesting food: NGOs and political mobilization in Europe. In C. K. Ansell & D. Vogel, eds., *What's the Beef? The Contested Governance of European Food Safety*. Cambridge, MA: MIT Press, pp. 97–122.

Ansell, C. K., & Vogel, D. (Eds.). (2006). *What's the Beef? The Contested Governance of European Food Safety*. Cambridge, MA: MIT Press.

Aradau, C. (2010). Security that matters: Critical infrastructure and objects of protection. *Security Dialogue*, 41(5), 491–514.

Aradau, C. (2004) Security and the democratic scene. *Journal of International Relations and Development*, 7(4), 388–413.

Aradau, C., Lobo-Guerrero, L., & Van Munster, R. (2008). Security, technologies of risk, and the political: Guest editors' introduction. *Security Dialogue*, 39(2–3), 147–154.

Asher, R. (2014). Organized labor and the origins of the Occupational Safety and Health Act. *New Solutions*, 24(3), 279–301.

Attanasio, David L. (2015). *The State Obligation to Protect*. PhD. Dissertation. UCLA.

Atwood, K., Colditz, G. A., & Kawachi, I. (1997). From public health science to prevention policy: Placing science in its social and political contexts. *American Journal of Public Health*, 87(10), 1603–1606.

Auriel, P. 2018. Introduction. In P. Auriel, O. Beaud, & C. Wellman, eds., *The Rule of Crisis: Terrorism, Emergency Legislation and the Rule of Law* (Vol. 64). Cham, Switzerland: Springer International Publishing, pp. 1–11.

Ayre, P. (2001). Child protection and the media: Lessons from the last three decades. *British Journal of Social Work*, 31(6), 887–901.

Balkin, J. M. (2008). The constitution in the national surveillance state. *Minnesota Law Review*, 93, 1–25.

Balzacq, T. (2008). The policy tools of securitization: Information exchange, EU foreign and interior policies. *Journal of Common Market Studies*, 46(1), 75–100.

Bardach, E., & Kagan, R. A. (2002). *Going by the Book: The Problem of Regulatory Unreasonableness*. New Brunswick, NJ: Transaction Publishers.

Baumgartner, F. R., & Jones, B. D. (1991). Agenda dynamics and policy subsystems. *The Journal of Politics*, 53(4), 1044–1074.

Beamish, T. D. (2002). Waiting for crisis: Regulatory inaction and ineptitude and the Guadalupe Dunes oil spill. *Social Problems*, 49(2), 150–177.

Beck, U. (1992). *Risk Society: Towards a New Modernity*. Thousand Oaks, CA: Sage.

Beermann, J. M. (2015). *NFIB* v. *Sebelius* and the right to health care: Government's obligation to provide for the health, safety and welfare of its citizens. *Journal of Legislation and Public Policy*, 18(2), 277–303.

Béland, D. (2005). Insecurity, citizenship, and globalization: The multiple faces of state protection. *Sociological Theory*, 23(1), 25–41.

Bellamy, A. J. (2010). The responsibility to protect – five years on. *Ethics & International Affairs*, 24(2), 143–169.

Beniger, J. (2009). *The Control Revolution: Technological and Economic Origins of the Information Society*. Cambridge, MA: Harvard University Press.

Bennett, C. J. (1988). Different processes, one result: The convergence of data protection policy in Europe and the United States. *Governance*, 1(4), 415–441.

Berg, M., & Geyer, M. H. (Eds.). (2002). *Two Cultures of Rights: The Quest for Inclusion and Participation in Modern America and Germany*. Cambridge: Cambridge University Press.

Berger, S. (Ed.). (1983). *Organizing Interests in Western Europe: Pluralism, Corporatism, and the Transformation of Politics*. Cambridge: Cambridge University Press.

Berns, N. S. (2017). *Framing the Victim: Domestic Violence, Media, and Social Problems*. Abingdon: Routledge.

Bigo, D. (2006). Internal and external aspects of security. *European Security*, 15(4), 385–404.

Binns, C. W., Lee, M. K., & Lee, A. H. (2018). Problems and prospects: Public health regulation of dietary supplements. *Annual Review of Public Health*, 39, 403–420.

Birkland, T. A. (1997). *After Disaster: Agenda Setting, Public Policy, and Focusing Events*. Washington, DC: Georgetown University Press.

Birkland, T. A., & Lawrence, R. G. (2009). Media framing and policy change after Columbine. *American Behavioral Scientist*, 52(10), 1405–1425.

Bishop, B. H. (2014). Focusing events and public opinion: Evidence from the Deepwater Horizon disaster. *Political Behavior*, 36(1), 1–22.

Bogard, C. J. (2001). Claimsmakers and contexts in early constructions of homelessness: A comparison of New York City and Washington, DC. *Symbolic Interaction*, 24(4), 425–454.

Boin, A. et al. (2014). *Civil Security and the European Union: A Survey of European Civil Security Systems and the Role of the EU in Building Shared Crisis Management Capacities*. UI Papers, #2. Stockholm: Swedish Institute of International Affairs, pp. 1–16.

Boin, A., 't Hart, P., & McConnell, A. (2009). Crisis exploitation: Political and policy impacts of framing contests. *Journal of European Public Policy*, 16(1), 81–106.

Bolsen, T., & Druckman, J. N. (2015). Counteracting the politicization of science. *Journal of Communication*, 65(5), 745–769.

Booth, R. W., Sharma, D., & Leader, T. I. (2016). The age of anxiety? It depends where you look: Changes in STAI trait anxiety, 1970–2010. *Social Psychiatry and Psychiatric Epidemiology*, 51(2), 193–202.

Boothe, K., & Harrison, K. (2009). The influence of institutions on issue definition: Children's environmental health policy in the United States and Canada. *Journal of Comparative Policy Analysis*, 11(3), 287–307.

Böschen, S., Kastenhofer, K., Rust, I., Soentgen, J., & Wehling, P. (2010). Scientific nonknowledge and its political dynamics: The cases of agri-biotechnology and mobile phoning. *Science, Technology, & Human Values*, 35(6), 783–811.

Boyd, D. R. (2011). *The Environmental Rights Revolution: A Global Study of Constitutions, Human Rights, and the Environment*. Vancouver: UBC Press.

Braithwaite, J. (2000). The new regulatory state and the transformation of criminology. *British Journal of Criminology*, 40(2), 222–238.

Brasoveanu, I. V., Brasoveanu, L. O., & Mascu, S. (2014). Comparative analysis of the consumer protection, considering the globalisation and technological changes, within member states of the European Union. *Amfiteatru Economic*, 16(36), 517.

Brown, E. K., & Socia, K. M. (2016). Twenty-first century punitiveness: Social sources of punitive American views reconsidered. *Journal of Quantitative Criminology*, 33(4), 935–959.

Brown, T. M., & Fee, E. (2014). Social movements in health. *Annual Review of Public Health*, 35, 385–398.

Brown, W. (1995). *States of Injury: Power and Freedom in Late Modernity*. Princeton, NJ: Princeton University Press.

Bubeck, P., Kreibich, H., Penning-Rowsell, E. C., Botzen, W. J. W., De Moel, H., & Klijn, F. (2017). Explaining differences in flood management approaches in Europe and in the USA – A comparative analysis. *Journal of Flood Risk Management*, 10(4), 436–445.

Butler, C., & Pidgeon, N. (2011). From "flood defence" to "flood risk management": Exploring governance, responsibility, and blame. *Environment and Planning C: Government and Policy*, 29(3), 533–547.

Butler, S., Elmeland, K., Thom, B., & Nicholls, J. (2017). *Alcohol, Power and Public Health: A Comparative Study of Alcohol Policy.* Milton Park, UK: Taylor & Francis.

Caduff, C. (2015). *The Pandemic Perhaps: Dramatic Events in a Public Culture of Danger.* Berkeley: University of California Press.

Campbell, L. (2014). Organized crime and national security. *New Criminal Law Review: In International and Interdisciplinary Journal,* 17(2), 220–251.

Carpenter, C. R. (2005). "Women, children and other vulnerable groups": Gender, strategic frames and the protection of civilians as a transnational issue. *International Studies Quarterly,* 49(2), 295–334.

Carpenter, D. P. (2014). *Reputation and Power: Organizational Image and Pharmaceutical Regulation at the FDA.* Princeton, NJ: Princeton University Press.

Carpenter, D. P. (2001). *The Forging of Bureaucratic Autonomy: Reputations, Networks, and Policy Innovation in Executive Agencies, 1862–1928.* Princeton, NJ: Princeton University Press.

Carpenter, D., & Sin, G. (2007). Policy tragedy and the emergence of regulation: The Food, Drug, and Cosmetic Act of 1938. *Studies in American Political Development,* 21(2), 149–180.

Cate, F. H. (1994). The EU data protection directive, information privacy, and the public interest. *Iowa Law Review,* 80, 431–443.

Chandler, D. (2013). International statebuilding and the ideology of resilience. *Politics,* 33(4), 276–286.

Charles, N., & Mackay, F. (2013). Feminist politics and framing contests: Domestic violence policy in Scotland and Wales. *Critical Social Policy,* 33(4), 593–615.

Charnysh, V., Lloyd, P., & Simmons, B. A. (2015). Frames and consensus formation in international relations: The case of trafficking in persons. *European Journal of International Relations,* 21(2), 323–351.

Chenot, D. (2011). The vicious cycle: Recurrent interactions among the media, politicians, the public, and child welfare services organizations. *Journal of Public Child Welfare,* 5(2–3), 167–184.

Christensen, T., & Lægreid, P. (2007). The whole-of-government approach to public sector reform. *Public Administration Review,* 67(6), 1059–1066.

Christensen, T., & Lodge, M. (2018). Reputation management in societal security: A comparative study. *The American Review of Public Administration,* 48(2), 119–132.

Chuang, J. (2006). Beyond a snapshot: Preventing human trafficking in the global economy. *Indiana Journal of Global Legal Studies,* 13(1), 137–163.

Clarke, L. (2006). *Worst Cases: Terror and Catastrophe in the Popular Imagination*. Chicago: University of Chicago Press.

Cmiel, K. (2004). The recent history of human rights. *The American Historical Review*, 109(1), 117–135.

Coaffee, J. (2013). Rescaling and responsibilising the politics of urban resilience: From national security to local place-making. *Politics*, 33(4), 240–252.

Coaffee, J., & Fussey, P. (2015). Constructing resilience through security and surveillance: The politics, practices and tensions of security-driven resilience. *Security Dialogue*, 46(1), 86–105.

Cobb, R. W., & Primo, D. M. (2003). *The Plane Truth: Airline Crashes, the Media, and Transportation Policy*. Washington, DC: Brookings Institution Press.

Cohen, L. (2003). *A Consumers' Republic*. New York: Alfred A. Knopf.

Coleman, W. D., Skogstad, G. D., & Atkinson, M. M. (1996). Paradigm shifts and policy networks: Cumulative change in agriculture. *Journal of Public Policy*, 16(3), 273–301.

Collier, S. J. (2014). Neoliberalism and natural disaster: Insurance as political technology of catastrophe. *Journal of Cultural Economy*, 7(3), 273–290.

Collier, S. J., & Lakoff, A. (2015). Vital systems security: Reflexive biopolitics and the government of emergency. *Theory, Culture & Society*, 32(2), 19–51.

Collier, S., & Lakoff, A. (2008). The vulnerability of vital systems: How "critical infrastructure" became a security problem. In M. Dunn & K. Kristensen, eds., *Securing the Homeland: Critical Infrastructure, Risk and (In) security*. Abingdon: Routledge, pp. 40–62.

Conrad, P. (2007). *The Medicalization of Society*. Baltimore: Johns Hopkins University Press.

Cordner, A., Mulcahy, M., & Brown, P. (2013). Chemical regulation on fire: Rapid policy advances on flame retardants. *Environmental Science & Technology*, 47(13), 7067–7076.

Critcher, C. (2011). For a political economy of moral panics. *Crime, Media, Culture*, 7(3), 259–275.

Cuéllar, M. F. (2009). "Securing" the nation: Law, politics, and organization at the Federal Security Agency, 1939–1953. *University of Chicago Law Review*, 76(2), 587–718.

Curley, T. M. (2015). Models of emergency statebuilding in the United States. *Perspectives on Politics*, 13(3), 697–713.

Daemmrich, A. A. (2004). *Pharmacopolitics: Drug Regulation in the United States and Germany*. Philadelphia: Chemical Heritage Foundation.

Daugbjerg, C. (1998). Linking policy networks and environmental policies: Nitrate policy making in Denmark and Sweden 1970–1995. *Public Administration*, 76(2), 275–294.

Dekker, J. J. (2010). Child maltreatment in the last 50 years: The use of statistics. In P. Smeyers & M. Depaepe, eds., *Educational Research – The Ethics and Aesthetics of Statistics*. Dordrecht: Springer, pp. 43–57.

De Grazia, V. (2009). *Irresistible Empire: America's Advance through Twentieth-Century Europe*. Cambridge, MA: Harvard University Press.

Dekker, S. (2017). *The End of Heaven: Disaster and Suffering in a Scientific Age*. Abingdon: Routledge.

Demeritt, D., Rothstein, H., Beaussier, A. L., & Howard, M. (2015). Mobilizing risk: Explaining policy transfer in food and occupational safety regulation in the UK. *Environment and Planning A*, 47(2), 373–391.

Dickens, M. (2014). Safe until proven unsafe: Solving the growing debate around dietary supplement regulation. *Wake Forest Journal of Business and Intellectual Property Law*, 15(4), 576–597.

Dingwall, R., & Frost, S. (Eds.). (2017). *Health and Safety in a Changing World*. Milton Park, UK: Taylor & Francis.

Donzelot, J. (1977). *The Policing of Families*. Baltimore: John Hopkins University Press.

Douglas, E. M. (2009). Media coverage of agency-related child maltreatment fatalities: Does it result in state legislative change intended to prevent future fatalities? *Journal of Policy Practice*, 8(3), 224–239.

Dove, L. R. (2013). A constitutional right to police protection and classical liberal theory: Complement, not conflict. *Akron Journal of Constitutional Law and Policy*, 4, 37–69.

Duffy, J. (1992). *The Sanitarians: A History of American Public Health*. Chicago: University of Illinois Press.

Dunn, E. (2007). Escherichia coli, corporate discipline and the failure of the sewer state. *Space and Polity*, 11(1), 35–53.

Dunn, J. L. (2005). "Victims" and "survivors": Emerging vocabularies of motive for "battered" women who stay. *Sociological Inquiry*, 75(1), 1–30.

Dworkin, G. (1972). Paternalism. *The Monist*, 56(1), 64–84.

Edwards, F. (2016). Saving children, controlling families: Punishment, redistribution, and child protection. *American Sociological Review*, 81(3), 575–595.

Eilperin, J., Dennis, B., & Mooney, C. (2018, Oct. 1). Government report reveals the Trump Administration Is fully aware of the devastating impacts of climate change. *The Washington Post*. Available from www.sciencealert.com/government-report-reveals-the-trump-administration-is-already-preparing-for-the-worst-when-it-comes-to-climate-change#

Elbe, S. (2012). Bodies as battlefields: Toward the medicalization of insecurity. *International Political Sociology*, 6(3), 320–322.

Elman, R. A. (1996). *Sexual Subordination and State Intervention: Comparing Sweden and the United States*. New York: Berghahn Books.

Epp, C. R. (2010). *Making Rights Real: Activists, Bureaucrats, and the Creation of the Legalistic State*. Chicago: University of Chicago Press.

Epp, C. R. (1998). *The Rights Revolution: Lawyers, Activists, and Supreme Courts in Comparative Perspective*. Chicago: University of Chicago Press.

Esping-Andersen, G. (2013). *The Three Worlds of Welfare Capitalism*. Hoboken, NJ: John Wiley & Sons.

Epstein, R. A. (1995). The harm principle - and how it grew. *The University of Toronto Law Journal*, 45(4), 369–417.

Epstein, S. (2016). The politics of health mobilization in the United States: The promise and pitfalls of "disease constituencies." *Social Science & Medicine*, 165, 246–254.

Epstein, S. (2008). Patient groups and health movements. In E. Hackett, O. Amsterdamska, M. Lynch, & J. Wacjman, eds., *The Handbook of Science and Technology Studies*. Cambridge, MA: MIT Press, pp. 499–539.

Esbester, M., & Almond, P. (2017). Do the public have a problem with health and safety? In R. Dingwall & S. Frost, eds., *Health and Safety in a Changing World*. London: Routledge, pp. 16–35.

Escobar, M. P., & Demeritt, D. (2014). Flooding and the framing of risk in British broadsheets, 1985–2010. *Public Understanding of Science*, 23(4), 454–471.

Esmark, A. (2018). Limits to liberal government: An alternative history of governmentality. *Administration & Society*, 50(2), 240–268.

Evans, E. (2010). Constitutional inclusion of animal rights in Germany and Switzerland: How did animal protection become an issue of national importance? *Society & Animals*, 18(3), 231–250.

Ewald, F. (2014). *L'Etat Providence*. Paris: Grasset.

Ewald, F. (1999). The return of the crafty genius: An outline of a philosophy of precaution. *Connecticut Insurance Law Journal*, 6, 47–79.

Ezrahi, Y. (1990). *The Descent of Icarus: Science and the Transformation of Contemporary Democracy*. Cambridge, MA: Harvard University Press.

Fairchild, A. L., Rosner, D., Colgrove, J., Bayer, R., & Fried, L. P. (2010). The EXODUS of public health: What history can tell us about the future. *American Journal of Public Health*, 100(1), 54–63.

Fangerau, H., Görgen, A., & Griemmert, M. (2015). Child welfare and child protection: Medicalization and scandalization as the new norms in dealing with violence against children. In A. Bagattini & C. Macleod, eds., *The Nature of Children's Well-Being*. Dordrecht: Springer, pp. 209–225

Feeley, M. M., & Simon, J. (1992). The new penology: Notes on the emerging strategy of corrections and its implications. *Criminology*, 30(4), 449–474.

Feurer, R. (1988). The meaning of "sisterhood": The British women's movement and protective labor legislation, 1870–1900. *Victorian Studies*, 31(2), 233–260.

Fleming, A. K., Rutledge, P. E., Dixon, G. C., & Peralta, J. S. (2016). When the smoke clears: Focusing events, issue definition, strategic framing, and the politics of gun control. *Social Science Quarterly*, 97(5), 1144–1156.

Flickinger, R. (1983). The comparative politics of agenda setting: The emergence of consumer protection as a public policy issue in Britain and the United States. *Review of Policy Research*, 2(3), 429–444.

Foucault, M. (2012). *Discipline and Punish: The Birth of the Prison*. New York: Vintage Books.

France, A., & Utting, D. (2005). The paradigm of "risk and protection-focused prevention" and its impact on services for children and families. *Children & Society*, 19(2), 77–90.

Frewer, L. J., Miles, S., & Marsh, R. (2002). The media and genetically modified foods: Evidence in support of social amplification of risk. *Risk Analysis: An International Journal*, 22(4), 701–711.

Friedman, B. H. (2011). Managing fear: The politics of homeland security. *Political Science Quarterly*, 126(1), 77–106.

Friedman, D. A. (2013). Public health regulation and the limits of paternalism. *Connecticut. Law Review*, 46(5), 1687–1770.

Friedman, D. A. (2007). Reinventing consumer protection. *DePaul Law Review*, 57, 45–91.

Friedman, L. M. (1994). *Total Justice*. New York: Russell Sage Foundation.

Friedman, L. M., & Thompson, J. (2003). Total disaster and total justice: Responses to man-made tragedy. *DePaul Law Review*, 53, 251–287.

Friesendorf, C. (2007). Pathologies of security governance: Efforts against human trafficking in Europe. *Security Dialogue*, 38(3), 379–402.

Furedi, F. (2009). Precautionary culture and the rise of possibilistic risk assessment. *Erasmus Law Review*, 2(2), 197–220.

Furedi, F. (2005). *Politics of Fear*. London: A&C Black.

Gainsborough, J. F. (2009). Scandals, lawsuits, and politics: Child welfare policy in the US States. *State Politics & Policy Quarterly*, 9(3), 325–355.

Garland, D. (2003). The rise of risk. In R. V. Erickson & A. Doyle, eds., *Risk and Morality*. Toronto: University of Toronto Press, pp. 48–86.

Garland, D. (2001). *The Culture of Control: Crime and Social Order in Contemporary Society*. Chicago: University of Chicago Press.

Gauchat, G. (2012). Politicization of science in the public sphere: A study of public trust in the United States, 1974 to 2010. *American Sociological Review*, 77(2), 167–187.

Giddens, A. (1999). Risk and responsibility. *The Modern Law Review*, 62(1), 1–10.

Gilbert, N. (2012). A comparative study of child welfare systems: Abstract orientations and concrete results. *Children and Youth Services Review*, 34(3), 532–536.

Gilbert, N. (2002). *Transformation of the Welfare State: The Silent Surrender of Public Responsibility*. New York: Oxford University Press.

Glassner, B. (1999). *The Culture of Fear*. New York: Basic Books.

Glickman, L. B. (2001). The strike in the temple of consumption: Consumer activism and twentieth-century American political culture. *The Journal of American History*, 88(1), 99–128.

Gormley Jr., W. T. (1986). Regulatory issue networks in a federal system. *Polity*, 18(4), 595–620.

Gostin, L. O., & Gostin, K. G. (2009). A broader liberty: JS Mill, paternalism and the public's health. *Public Health*, 123(3), 214–221.

Gourevitch, A. (2010). Environmentalism – long live the politics of fear. *Public Culture*, 22(3), 411–424.

Gray, G. C. (2009). The responsibilization strategy of health and safety: Neo-liberalism and the reconfiguration of individual responsibility for risk. *The British Journal of Criminology*, 49(3), 326–342.

Green, J. (1997). *Risk and Misfortune: A Social Construction of Accidents*. Milton Park, UK: Taylor & Francis.

Gross, M. L., Canetti, D., & Vashdi, D. R. (2017). Cyberterrorism: Its effects on psychological well-being, public confidence and political attitudes. *Journal of Cybersecurity*, 3(1), 49–58.

Grüning, T., Strünck, C., & Gilmore, A. B. (2008). Puffing away? Explaining the politics of tobacco control in Germany. *German Politics*, 17(2), 140–164.

Guillén, M. F., & Capron, L. (2016). State capacity, minority shareholder protections, and stock market development. *Administrative Science Quarterly*, 61(1), 125–160.

Guldbrandsson, K., & Fossum, B. (2009). An exploration of the theoretical concepts policy windows and policy entrepreneurs at the Swedish public health arena. *Health Promotion International*, 24(4), 434–444.

Hagmann, J., & Cavelty, M. D. (2012). National risk registers: Security scientism and the propagation of permanent insecurity. *Security Dialogue*, 43(1), 79–96.

Hainmüller, J., & Lemnitzer, J. M. (2003). Why do Europeans fly safer? The politics of airport security in Europe and the US. *Terrorism and Political Violence*, 15(4), 1–36.

Hallsworth, S., & Lea, J. (2011). Reconstructing Leviathan: Emerging contours of the security state. *Theoretical Criminology*, 15(2), 141–157.

Halpin, H. A., Morales-Suárez-Varela, M. M., & Martin-Moreno, J. M. (2010). Chronic disease prevention and the new public health. *Public Health Reviews*, 32(1), 120.

Hammit, J., Rogers, M., Sand, P., & Wiener, J. B. (2013). *The Reality of Precaution: Comparing Risk Regulation in the United States and Europe*. Abingdon: Routledge.

Hanrieder, T., & Kreuder-Sonnen, C. (2014). WHO decides on the exception? Securitization and emergency governance in global health. *Security Dialogue*, 45(4), 331–348.

Harcourt, B. E. (1999). The collapse of the harm principle. *Journal of Criminal Law & Criminology*, 90(1), 109–193.

Hardy, C., & Maguire, S. (2016). Organizing risk: Discourse, power, and "riskification." *Academy of Management Review*, 41(1), 80–108.

Harris, D. A. (2005). *Good Cops: The Case for Preventive Policing*. New York: The New Press.

Harrison, K. (1995). Is cooperation the answer? Canadian environmental enforcement in comparative context. *Journal of Policy Analysis and Management*, 14(2), 221–244.

Hearn, J., Strid, S., Husu, L., & Verloo, M. (2016). Interrogating violence against women and state violence policy: Gendered intersectionalities and the quality of policy in The Netherlands, Sweden and the UK. *Current Sociology*, 64(4), 551–567.

Hebenton, B., & Seddon, T. (2009). From dangerousness to precaution: Managing sexual and violent offenders in an insecure and uncertain age. *The British Journal of Criminology*, 49(3), 343–362.

Heclo, H. (1978). Issue networks and the executive establishment. In R. Stillman, ed., *Public Administration Concepts and Cases*. New York: Barnes and Noble, pp. 46–57.

Hemerijck, A. (2012). Two or three waves of welfare state transformation? In N. Morel, B. Palier, & J. Palme, eds., *Towards a Social Investment Welfare State?* Bristol, UK: The Policy Press, pp. 33–60.

Heyer, K. C. (2002). The ADA on the road: Disability frights in Germany. *Law & Social Inquiry*, 27(4), 723–762.

Heyman, S. J. (1991). First duty of government: Protection, liberty and the Fourteenth Amendment. *Duke Law Journal*, 41, 507–571.

Hier, S. P., Lett, D., Walby, K., & Smith, A. (2011). Beyond folk devil resistance: Linking moral panic and moral regulation. *Criminology and Criminal Justice*, 11(3), 259–276.

Hilton, M. (2009). *Prosperity for All: Consumer Activism in an Era of Globalization*. Ithaca: Cornell University Press.

Hilton, M. (2007). Social activism in an age of consumption: The organized consumer movement. *Social History*, 32(2), 121–143.

Howlett, M. (2002). Do networks matter? Linking policy network structure to policy outcomes: Evidence from four Canadian policy sectors 1990–2000. *Canadian Journal of Political Science/Revue Canadienne de Science Politique*, 35(2), 235–267.

Howlett, M., & Ramesh, M. (1998). Policy subsystem configurations and policy change: Operationalizing the postpositivist analysis of the politics of the policy process. *Policy Studies Journal*, 26(3), 466–481.

Htun, M., & Weldon, S. L. (2012). The civic origins of progressive policy change: Combating violence against women in global perspective, 1975–2005. *American Political Science Review*, 106(3), 548–569.

Huber, P. M. (2008). Risk decisions in German constitutional and administrative law. In G. Woodman & D. Klippel, eds., *Risk and the Law*. Abingdon: Routledge, pp. 35–47.

Huffman, M. K. (2016). Moral panic and the politics of fear: The dubious logic underlying sex offender registration statutes and proposals for restoring measures of judicial discretion to sex offender management. *Virginia Journal of Criminal Law*, 4(2), 241–303.

Hurka, S., & Nebel, K. (2013). Framing and policy change after shooting rampages: A comparative analysis of discourse networks. *Journal of European Public Policy*, 20(3), 390–406.

Hutter, G., Leibenath, M., & Mattissek, A. (2014). Governing through resilience? Exploring flood protection in Dresden, Germany. *Social Sciences*, 3(2), 272–287.

Huysmans, J. (2004). Minding exceptions: The politics of insecurity and liberal democracy. *Contemporary Political Theory*, 3(3), 321–341.

Ignatieff, M. (2007). *The Rights Revolution*. Toronto: House of Anansi.

Iriye, A., Goedde, P., & Hitchcock, W. I. (Eds.). (2012). *The Human Rights Revolution: An International History* (Vol. 3). Oxford: Oxford University Press.

Iyengar, S. (1990). Framing responsibility for political issues: The case of poverty. *Political Behavior*, 12(1), 19–40.

Jagannathan, R., & Camasso, M. J. (2011). The crucial role played by social outrage in efforts to reform child protective services. *Children and Youth Services Review*, 33(6), 894–900.

Jansson, M. (2009). Feeding children and protecting women: The emergence of breastfeeding as an international concern. *Women's Studies International Forum*, 32(3), 240–248.

Janus, E. S. (2006). *Failure to Protect: America's Sexual Predator Laws and the Rise of the Preventive State*. Ithaca: Cornell University Press.

Jasanoff, S. (2011). *Designs on Nature: Science and Democracy in Europe and the United States*. Princeton, NJ: Princeton University Press.

Jasanoff, S. (1998). The political science of risk perception. *Reliability Engineering & System Safety*, 59(1), 91–99.

Jasanoff, S. (1990). *The Fifth Branch: Science Advisers as Policymakers*. Cambridge, MA: Harvard University Press.

Jenkins, P. (1994). "The ice age" the social construction of a drug panic. *Justice Quarterly*, 11(1), 7–31.

Jennings, B. (2007). Public health and civic republicanism: Toward an alternative framework for public health ethics. In A. Dawson & M. Verweij, eds., *Ethics, Prevention and Public Health*. Oxford: Oxford University Press, pp. 30–58.

Jensen, C. (2011). Focusing events, policy dictators and the dynamics of reform. *Policy Studies*, 32(2), 143–158.

Jenson, J. (1989). Paradigms and political discourse: Protective legislation in France and the United States before 1914. *Canadian Journal of Political Science*, 22(2), 235–258.

Jeon, Y., & Haider-Markel, D. P. (2001). Tracing issue definition and policy change: An analysis of disability issue images and policy response. *Policy Studies Journal*, 29(2), 215–231.

Joachim, J. (2003). Framing issues and seizing opportunities: The UN, NGOs, and women's rights. *International Studies Quarterly*, 47(2), 247–274.

Jochim, A. E., & May, P. J. (2010). Beyond subsystems: Policy regimes and governance. *Policy Studies Journal*, 38(2), 303–327.

Johnson, C. L., Tunstall, S.M., & Penning-Rowsell, E. C. (2005). Floods as catalysts for policy change: Historical lessons from England and Wales. *Water Resources Development*, 21(4), 561–575.

Johnson, G. F. (2007). Discursive democracy in the transgenerational context and a precautionary turn in public reasoning. *Contemporary Political Theory*, 6(1), 67–85.

Joly, P. B. (2007). Scientific expertise in public arenas: Lessons from the French experience. *Journal of Risk Research*, 10(7), 905–924.

Jones, M. M., & Bayer, R. (2007). Paternalism & its discontents: Motorcycle helmet laws, libertarian values, and public health. *American Journal of Public Health*, 97(2), 208–217.

Joseph, J. (2013). Resilience as embedded neoliberalism: A governmentality approach. *Resilience*, 1(1), 38–52.

Kagan, R. (2009). *Adversarial Legalism: The American Way of Law*. Cambridge, MA: Harvard University Press.

Kagan, R. (2000). Introduction: Comparing national styles of regulation in Japan and the United States. *Law & Policy*, 22(3–4), 225–244.

Kamradt-Scott, A. (2012). Changing perceptions: Of pandemic influenza and public health responses. *American Journal of Public Health*, 102(1), 90–98.

Kasperson, R. E., & Kasperson, J. X. (1996). The social amplification and attenuation of risk. *The Annals of the American Academy of Political and Social Science*, 545(1), 95–105.

Kastner, L. (2017). Tracing policy influence of diffuse interests: The post-crisis consumer finance protection politics in the US. *Journal of Civil Society*, 13(2), 130–148.

Keiser, K. R. (1980). The new regulation of health and safety. *Political Science Quarterly*, 95(3), 479–491.

Keller, A. C. (2009). *Science in Environmental Policy: The Politics of Objective Advice*. Cambridge, MA: MIT Press.

Keller, A. C., & Packel, L. (2014). Going for the cure: Patient interest groups and health advocacy in the United States. *Journal of Health Politics, Policy and Law*, 39(2), 331–367.

Kelman, S. (1981). *Regulating America. Regulating Sweden: A Comparative Study of Occupational Safety and Health Policy*. Cambridge, MA: MIT Press.

Kemshall, H. (2002). *Risk, Social Policy and Welfare*. New York: McGraw-Hill Education.

Kerr, O. S. (2009). The national surveillance state: A response to Balkin. *Minnesota Law Review Headnotes*, 93, 2179–2184.

Kersh, R., & Morone, J. A. (2005). Obesity, courts, and the new politics of public health. *Journal of Health Politics, Policy and Law*, 30(5), 839–868.

Kersh, R., & Morone, J. A. (2002). How the personal becomes political: Prohibitions, public health, and obesity. *Studies in American Political Development*, 16(2), 162–175.

Kete, K. (2002). Animals and ideology: The politics of animal protection in Europe. In N. Rothfels, ed., *Representing Animals*. Bloomington: Indiana University Press, pp. 17–34.

Kickbusch, I. (2003). The contribution of the World Health Organization to a new public health and health promotion. *American Journal of Public Health*, 93(3), 383–388.

Kingdon, J. W. (1984). *Agendas, Alternatives, and Public Policies*. Boston: Little, Brown.

Kitzinger, J. (1999). Researching risk and the media. *Health, Risk & Society,* 1(1), 55–69.

Klinke, A., & Renn, O. (2018). Distributed responsibility in risk governance. In P. A. Wilderer, O. Renn, M. Grambow, M. Molls, & K. Mainzer, eds., *Sustainable Risk Management.* Cham, Switzerland: Springer, pp. 19–31.

Klinke, A., & Renn, O. (2002). A new approach to risk evaluation and management: Risk-based, precaution-based, and discourse-based strategies. *Risk Analysis,* 22(6), 1071–1094.

Knowles, S. G. (2012). *The Disaster Experts: Mastering Risk in Modern America.* Philadelphia: University of Pennsylvania Press.

Krieger, K. (2013). The limits and variety of risk-based governance: The case of flood management in Germany and England. *Regulation & Governance,* 7(2), 236–257.

Kurzer, P., & Cooper, A. (2011). Hold the croissant! The European Union declares war on obesity. *Journal of European Social Policy,* 21(2), 107–119.

Kysar, D. A. (2006). It might have been: Risk, precaution and opportunity costs. *Journal of Land Use & Environmental Law,* 22, 1–57.

Lægreid, P., & Rykkja, L. H. (Eds.). (2019). *Societal Security and Crisis.* Cham, Switzerland: Palgrave Macmillan.

Lancaster, K., Ritter, A., & Colebatch, H. (2014). Problems, policy and politics: Making sense of Australia's "ice epidemic." *Policy Studies,* 35(2), 147–171.

Landy, M. K. (1995). The new politics of environmental policy. In M. K. Landy & M. A. Levin, eds., *The New Politics of Public Policy.* Baltimore: Johns Hopkins University Press, pp. 207–227.

Landy, M. K., & Levin, M. A. (Eds.). (1995). *The New Politics of Public Policy.* Baltimore. Johns Hopkins University Press.

Lango, P., Rykkja, L. H., & Lægreid, P. (2011). Organizing for Internal Security and Safety in Norway, Risk Management Trends, Giancarlo Nota, IntechOpen, DOI:10.5772/18277. Available from www.intechopen.com /books/risk-management-trends/organizing-for-internal-security-and-safety-in-norway

Lau, R. W. (2009). The contemporary culture of blame and the fetishization of the modernist mentality. *Current Sociology,* 57(5), 661–683.

Lawrence, R. G. (2004). Framing obesity: The evolution of news discourse on a public health issue. *Harvard International Journal of Press/Politics,* 9(3), 56–75.

Lee, M. T. (1998). The Ford Pinto case and the development of auto safety regulations, 1893–1978. *Business and Economic History,* 27(2), 390–401.

Leggett, W. (2014). The politics of behaviour change: Nudge, neoliberalism and the state. *Policy & Politics,* 42(1), 3–19.

Lehrer, E. (2012). Strange bedfellows: Smartersafer.org and the Biggert-Waters Act of 2012. *Duke Environmental Law and Policy Forum*, 23, 351–361.

Leisering, L., & Mabbett, D. (2011). Introduction: Towards a new regulatory state in old-age security? Exploring the issues. In L. Leisering, ed., *The New Regulatory State*. Houndmills, UK: Palgrave Macmillan, pp. 1–28.

Leka, S., Jain, A., Zwetsloot, G., Andreou, N., & Hollis, D. (2017). The changing landscape of occupational health and safety policy in the UK. In R. Dingwall & S. Frost, eds., *Health and Safety in a Changing World*. Milton Park, UK: Taylor & Francis.

Lemke, T. (2001). "The birth of bio-politics": Michel Foucault's lecture at the Collège de France on neo-liberal governmentality. *Economy and Society*, 30(2), 190–207.

Lentzos, F., & Rose, N. (2009). Governing insecurity: Contingency planning, protection, resilience. *Economy and Society*, 38(2), 230–254.

Levenstein, H. (2012). *Fear of Food*. Chicago: University of Chicago Press.

Lijphart, A. (2012). *Democracies: Patterns of Majoritarian and Consensus Government in Thirty-Six Countries*. New Haven, CT: Yale University Press.

Linders, A., & Bogard, C. (2014). Teenage pregnancy as a social problem: A comparison of Sweden and the United States. In A. L. Cherry & M. L. Dillon, eds., *International Handbook of Adolescent Pregnancy*. Boston, MA: Springer, pp. 147–157.

Lindholm, J. (2017). Threat or opportunity? The politicization of focusing events in the parliamentary arena. *Journal of Contingencies and Crisis Management*, 25(2), 79–90.

Litfin, K. (1994). *Ozone Discourses: Science and Politics in Global Environmental Cooperation*. New York: Columbia University Press.

Lodge, M. (2011). Risk, regulation and crisis: Comparing national responses in food safety regulation. *Journal of Public Policy*, 31(1), 25–50.

Lodge, M., & Hood, C. (2002). Pavlovian policy responses to media feeding frenzies? Dangerous dogs regulation in comparative perspective. *Journal of Contingencies and Crisis Management*, 10(1), 1–13.

Lodge, M., & Wegrich, K. (2011). Governance as contested logics of control: Europeanized meat inspection regimes in Denmark and Germany. *Journal of European Public Policy*, 18(1), 90–105.

Lofstedt, R. E. (2011). Risk versus hazard – How to regulate in the 21st century. *European Journal of Risk Regulation*, 2(2), 149–168.

Lubitow, A. (2013). Collaborative frame construction in social movement campaigns: Bisphenol-A (BPA) and scientist–activist mobilization. *Social Movement Studies*, 12(4), 429–447.

Lundström, T. (2001). Child protection, voluntary organizations, and the public sector in Sweden. *Voluntas: International Journal of Voluntary and Nonprofit Organizations*, 12(4), 355–371.

Mackenbach, J. P., & McKee, M. (2013). A comparative analysis of health policy performance in 43 European countries. *The European Journal of Public Health*, 23(2), 195–201.

Mahoney, C. (2007). Networking vs. allying: The decision of interest groups to join coalitions in the US and the EU. *Journal of European Public Policy*, 14(3), 366–383.

Majone, G. (1997). From the positive to the regulatory state: Causes and consequences of changes in the mode of governance. *Journal of Public Policy*, 17(2), 139–167.

Majone, G. (1994). The rise of the regulatory state in Europe. *West European Politics*, 17(3), 77–101.

Mamudu, H. M., & Studlar, D. T. (2009). Multilevel governance and shared sovereignty: European Union, member states, and the FCTC. *Governance*, 22(1), 73–97.

Mansell, J., Ota, R., Erasmus, R., & Marks, K. (2011). Reframing child protection: A response to a constant crisis of confidence in child protection. *Children and Youth Services Review*, 33(11), 2076–2086.

Mares, I. (2003). *The Politics of Social Risk: Business and Welfare State Development*. Cambridge: Cambridge University Press.

Marsh, D., & Rhodes, R. A. W. (1992). *Policy Networks in British Government*. Oxford: Clarendon Press.

Marsh, D., & Smith, M. (2000). Understanding policy networks: Towards a dialectical approach. *Political Studies*, 48(1), 4–21.

Marshall, T. H., & Bottomore, T. B. (1992). *Citizenship and Social Class* (Vol. 2). London: Pluto Press.

Mascini, P., Achterberg, P., & Houtman, D. (2013). Neoliberalism and work-related risks: Individual or collective responsibilization? *Journal of Risk Research*, 16(10), 1209–1224.

Mayer, R. N. (1991). Gone yesterday, here today: Consumer issues in the agenda-setting process. *Journal of Social Issues*, 47(1), 21–39.

McBeth, M. K., Clemons, R. S., Husmann, M. A., Kusko, E., & Gaarden, A. (2013). The social construction of a crisis: Policy narratives and contemporary US obesity policy. *Risk, Hazards & Crisis in Public Policy*, 4(3), 135–163.

McEvoy, A. F. (1995). The Triangle Shirtwaist Factory Fire of 1911: Social change, industrial accidents, and the evolution of common-sense causality. *Law & Social Inquiry*, 20(2), 621–651.

Melnick, R. S. (1995). Separation of powers and the strategy of rights: The expansion of special education. In M. K., Landy & M. A. Levin, eds., *The New Politics of Public Policy*. Baltimore: Johns Hopkins University Press, pp. 23–46.

Mill, J. S. (1865). *On Liberty*. London: Longman, Greens and Co.

Mintrom, M., & Norman, P. (2009). Policy entrepreneurship and policy change. *Policy Studies Journal*, 37(4), 649–667.

Monkkonen, E. H. (1992). History of urban police. *Crime and Justice*, 15, 547–580.

Montpetit, E., & Rouillard, C. (2008). Culture and the democratization of risk management: The widening biotechnology gap between Canada and France. *Administration & Society*, 39(8), 907–930.

Moore, M., Yeatman, H., & Davey, R. (2015). Which nanny – the state or industry? Wowsers, teetotallers and the fun police in public health advocacy. *Public Health*, 129(8), 1030–1037.

Moss, D. A. (2004). *When All Else Fails: Government as the Ultimate Risk Manager*. Cambridge, MA: Harvard University Press.

Myers, J. E. (2008). A short history of child protection in America. *Family Law Quarterly*, 42(3), 449–463.

Nash, L. (2017). From safety to risk: The cold war contexts of American environmental policy. *Journal of Policy History*, 29(1), 1–33.

Nash, R. F. (1989). *The Rights of Nature: A History of Environmental Ethics*. Madison: University of Wisconsin Press.

Nathanson, C. A. (2007a). *Disease Prevention as Social Change: The State, Society, and Public Health in the United States, France, Great Britain, and Canada*. New York: Russell Sage Foundation.

Nathanson, C. A. (2007b). The contingent power of experts: Public health policy in the United States, Britain, and France. *Journal of Policy History*, 19(1), 71–94.

Nestle, M. (2013). *Food Politics: How the Food Industry Influences Nutrition and Health*. Berkeley: University of California Press.

Nestle, M. (2003). *Safe Food: Bacteria, Biotechnology, and Bioterrorism*. Berkeley: University of California Press.

Nielsen, M. E. J. (2011). Republicanism as a paradigm for public health – Some comments. *Public Health Ethics*, 4(1), 40–52.

Niemi, M. (2016). *Public Health and Municipal Policy Making: Britain and Sweden, 1900–1940*. Abingdon: Routledge.

Nolan Jr., J. L. (1998). *The Therapeutic State: Justifying Government at Century's End*. New York: New York University Press.

Novkov, J. (2001). *Constituting Workers, Protecting Women: Gender, Law and Labor in the Progressive Era and New Deal Years*. Ann Arbor: University of Michigan Press.

Nownes, A., & Neeley, G. (1996). Toward an explanation for public interest group formation and proliferation. *Policy Studies Journal*, 24(1), 74–92.

O'Donovan, K. (2017). An assessment of aggregate focusing events, disaster experience, and policy change. *Risk, Hazards & Crisis in Public Policy*, 8(3), 201–219.

Oliver, J. E. (2005). *Fat Politics: The Real Story behind America's Obesity Epidemic*. Oxford: Oxford University Press.

Oliver, T. R. (2006). The politics of public health policy. *Annual Review of Public Health*, 27, 195–233.

O'Malley, P. (2010). Resilient subjects: Uncertainty, warfare and liberalism. *Economy and Society*, 39(4), 488–509.

O'Malley, P. (2004). *Risk, Uncertainty and Government*. Milton Park, UK: Taylor and Francis.

O'Neil, P. D., & Krane, D. (2012). Policy and organizational change in the Federal Aviation Administration: The ontogenesis of a high-reliability organization. *Public Administration Review*, 72(1), 98–111.

Ong, A. (2006). *Neoliberalism as Exception: Mutations in Citizenship and Sovereignty*. Durham: Duke University Press.

Otto, S. K. (2005). State animal protection laws – The next generation. *Animal Law*, 11, 131–166.

Parton, N. (2010). "From dangerousness to risk": The growing importance of screening and surveillance systems for safeguarding and promoting the well-being of children in England. *Health, Risk & Society*, 12(1), 51–64.

Parton, N. (2008). The "Change for Children" programme in England: Towards the "preventive-surveillance state." *Journal of Law and Society*, 35(1), 166–187.

Parton, N. (1979). The natural history of child abuse: A study in social problem definition. *British Journal of Social Work*, 9(4), 431–451.

Patashnik, E. M., & Zelizer, J. E. (2013). The struggle to remake politics: Liberal reform and the limits of policy feedback in the contemporary American state. *Perspectives on Politics*, 11(4), 1071–1087.

Pearce, N. (1996). Traditional epidemiology, modern epidemiology, and public health. *American Journal of Public Health*, 86(5), 678–683.

Pedriana, N. (2006). From protective to equal treatment: Legal framing processes and transformation of the women's movement in the 1960s. *American Journal of Sociology*, 111(6), 1718–1761.

Peeters, R. (2015). The price of prevention: The preventative turn in crime policy and its consequences for the role of the state. *Punishment & Society*, 17(2), 163–183.

Peeters, R. (2013). *The Preventive Gaze: How Prevention Transforms Our Understanding of the State*. PhD Thesis. Tilburg University, Netherlands.

Penhale, B. (2007). Elder abuse in Europe: An overview of recent developments. *Journal of Elder Abuse & Neglect*, 18(1), 107–116.

Pettit, P. (2015). Freedom and the state: Nanny or nightwatchman? *Public Health*, 129(8), 1055 1060.

Pettit, P. (1987). Towards a social democratic theory of the state. *Political Studies*, 35(4), 537–551.

Pendas, D. O. (2012). Toward a new politics? On the recent historiography of human rights. *Contemporary European History*, 21(1), 95–111.

Petrunik, M., & Deutschmann, L. (2008). The exclusion–inclusion spectrum in state and community response to sex offenders in Anglo-American and European jurisdictions. *International Journal of Offender Therapy and Comparative Criminology*, 52(5), 499–519.

Pfohl, S. J. (1977). The "discovery" of child abuse. *Social Problems*, 24(3), 310–323.

Piller, C. (1991). *The Fail-Safe Society: Community Defiance and the End of American Technological Optimism*. New York: Basic Books.

Pope, T. M. (2003). Counting the dragon's teeth and claws: The definition of hard paternalism. *Georgia State University Law Review*, 20, 659–722.

Porter, D. (1999). *Health, Civilization, and the State: A History of Public Health from Ancient to Modern Times*. Abingdon: Psychology Press.

Pralle, S. (2006). The "mouse that roared": Agenda setting in Canadian pesticides politics. *Policy Studies Journal*, 34(2), 171–194.

Pratt, J., & Anderson, J. (2015). "The Beast of Blenheim," risk and the rise of the security sanction. *Australian & New Zealand Journal of Criminology*, 49(4), 528–545.

Princen, S. (2007). Advocacy coalitions and the internationalization of public health policies. *Journal of Public Policy*, 27(1), 13–33.

Pupavac, V. (2001). Therapeutic governance: Psycho-social intervention and trauma risk management. *Disasters*, 25(4), 358–372.

Reich, J. A. (2008). The child welfare system and state intervention in families: From historical patterns to future questions. *Sociology Compass*, 2(3), 888–909.

Ripstein, A. (2006). Beyond the harm principle. *Philosophy & Public Affairs*, 34(3), 215–245.

Roberts, P. S. (2013). *Disasters and the American State: How Politicians, Bureaucrats, and the Public Prepare for the Unexpected*. Cambridge: Cambridge University Press.

Rocco, P. (2015). Mapping the policy state. *Public Administration*, 93(1), 248–254.

Roe, P. (2012). Is securitization a "negative" concept? Revisiting the normative debate over normal versus extraordinary politics. *Security Dialogue*, 43(3), 249–266.

Rose, N., O'Malley, P., & Valverde, M. (2006). Governmentality. *Annual Review of Law and Social Science*, 2, 83–104.

Rosner, D., & Markowitz, G. (2016). Building the world that kills us: The politics of lead, science, and polluted homes, 1970 to 2000. *Journal of Urban History*, 42(2), 323–345.

Rothstein, H., Borraz, O., & Huber, M. (2013). Risk and the limits of governance: Exploring varied patterns of risk-based governance across Europe. *Regulation & Governance*, 7(2), 215–235.

Rothstein, H., Huber, M., & Gaskell, G. (2006). A theory of risk colonization: The spiralling regulatory logics of societal and institutional risk. *Economy and Society*, 35(1), 91–112.

Sack, E. J. (2004). Battered women and the state: The struggle for the future of domestic violence policy. *Wisconsin Law Review*, 6, 1657–1740.

Saetta, S. (2016). Medicalization of Sex Offenders: An Ethnological Study of a Specialized Prison and Treatment Facility in France. TEPSIS paper n°15 Réseau Monde Carcéral.

Saguy, A. C. (2000). Employment discrimination or sexual violence? Defining sexual harassment in American and French law. *Law and Society Review*, 34(4), 1091–1128.

Salter, M. B. (2008). Imagining numbers: Risk, quantification, and aviation security. *Security Dialogue*, 39(2–3), 243–266.

Sang-Hun, Choe (2016, Dec. 23). Korean court begins impeachment process. *New York Times*. Available from www.nytimes.com/2016/12/22/world/asia/south-korea-president-park-impeachment.html.

Scheberle, D. (1994). Radon and asbestos: A study of agenda setting and causal stories. *Policy Studies Journal*, 22(1), 74–86.

Schmitt, C. (1985). *Political Theology: Four Chapters on the Theory of Sovereignty*. Trans. George Schwab. Cambridge, MA: MIT Press.

Schwartz, V. E., & Silverman, C. (2005). Common-sense construction of consumer protection acts. *University of Kansas Law Review*, 54, 1–72.

Sell, T. K., Watson, C., Meyer, D., Kronk, M., Ravi, S., Pechta, L. E., Lubell K., & Rose, D. A. (2018). Frequency of risk-related news media messages in 2016 coverage of Zika virus. *Risk Analysis*, 38(12), 2514–2524.

Schou Tjalve, V. (2011). Designing (de)security: European exceptionalism, Atlantic republicanism and the "public sphere," *Security Dialogue*, 42(4–5), 441–452.

Scott, D. N. (2005). Shifting the burden of proof: The precautionary principle and its potential for the "democratization" of risk. Law Commission of Canada, 50–85.

Shapiro, S. A. (2014). Dying at work: Political discourse and occupational safety and health. *Wake Forest Law Review*, 49, 831–848.

Shapiro, S., & Glicksman, R. (2003). *Risk Regulation at Risk: Restoring a Pragmatic Approach*. Palo Alto: Stanford University Press.

Sheingate, A. (2012). Still a jungle. *Democracy*, 25, 48–59.

Shelton, D. (2015). Whiplash and backlash – Reflections on a human rights approach to environmental protection. *Santa Clara Journal of International Law*, 13, 11–30.

Shepard, B. (2007). Sex panic and the welfare state. *Journal of Sociology and Social Welfare*, 34, 155–172.

Shrader-Frechette, K. S. (1991). *Risk and Rationality: Philosophical Foundations for Populist Reforms*. Berkeley: University of California Press.

Simon, J. (1998). Managing the monstrous: Sex offenders and the new penology. *Psychology, Public Policy, and Law*, 4(1–2), 452–467.

Simon, J. (2005). Reversal of fortune: The resurgence of individual risk assessment in criminal justice. *Annual Review of Law and Social Science*, 1, 397–421.

Sjöberg, L. (2000). Factors in risk perception. *Risk Analysis*, 20(1), 1–12.

Skocpol, T. (1992). *Protecting Soldiers and Mothers*. Cambridge MA: Harvard University Press.

Skowronek, S. (2009). Taking stock. In L. Jacobs & D. King, eds., *The Unsustainable American State*. Oxford: Oxford University Press, pp. 330–338.

Skowronek, S. (1982). *Building a New American State: The Expansion of National Administrative Capacities, 1877–1920*. Cambridge: Cambridge University Press.

Skrentny, J. D. (2002). *The Minority Rights Revolution*. Cambridge, MA: Harvard University Press.

Slovic, P., Finucane, M. L., Peters, E., & MacGregor, D. G. (2004). Risk as analysis and risk as feelings: Some thoughts about affect, reason, risk, and rationality. *Risk Analysis*, 24(2), 311–322.

Slovic, P., Fischhoff, B., & Lichtenstein, S. (1986). The psychometric study of risk perception. In V. T. Covello, J. Menkes, & J. Mumpower, eds., *Risk Evaluation and Management*. New York: Plenum Press, pp. 3–24.

Small, S. D., & Barach, P. (2002). Patient safety and health policy: A history and review. *Hematology and Oncology Clinics of North America*, 16(6), 1463–1482.

Smith, M. J. (1991). From policy community to issue network: Salmonella in eggs and the new politics of food. *Public Administration*, 69(2), 235–255.

Sparrow, M. K. (2008). *The Character of Harms: Operational Challenges in Control*. Cambridge: Cambridge University Press.

Spicer, M.W., & Bowen, W.M. (2016). Are you scared yet? On the ethic of sustainability and the politics of fear in public administration. *Public Integrity*, 19(4), 300–315.

Stallings, R. A. (1990). Media discourse and the social construction of risk. *Social Problems*, 37(1), 80–95.

Starck, C. (2000). State duties of protection and fundamental rights. *Potchefstroom Electronic Law Journal/Potchefstroomse Elektroniese Regsblad*, 3(1), 1–51.

Stephenson, N., Davis, M., Flowers, P., MacGregor, C., & Waller, E. (2014). Mobilising "vulnerability" in the public health response to pandemic influenza. *Social Science & Medicine*, 102, 10–17.

Stolz, B. (2005). Educating policymakers and setting the criminal justice policymaking agenda: Interest groups and the "Victims of Trafficking and Violence Act of 2000." *Criminal Justice*, 5(4), 407–430.

Stone, D. A. (1989). Causal stories and the formation of policy agendas. *Political Science Quarterly*, 104(2), 281–300.

Storey, H. (2016). The meaning of "protection" within the refugee definition. *Refugee Survey Quarterly*, 35(3), 1–34.

Strünck, C. (2015). Consumer policy. In J. D. Wright, ed., *International Encyclopedia of the Social & Behavioral Sciences* (2nd ed., Vol. 4). Oxford: Elsevier, pp. 733–737.

Studlar, D. T. (2014). Cancer prevention through stealth: Science, policy advocacy, and multilevel governance in the establishment of a "National Tobacco Control Regime" in the United States. *Journal of Health Politics, Policy and Law*, 39(3), 503–535.

Sunstein, C. R. (2014). Nudging: A very short guide. *Journal of Consumer Policy*, 37(4), 583–588.

Sunstein, C. R. (2005). *Laws of Fear: Beyond the Precautionary Principle*. Cambridge: Cambridge University Press.

Sunstein, C. R. (2002a). The paralyzing principle. *Regulation*, 25, 32–37.

Sunstein, C. R. (2002b). *Risk and Reason: Safety, Law, and the Environment*. Cambridge: Cambridge University Press.

Sunstein, C. R., & Thaler, R. H. (2003). Libertarian paternalism is not an oxymoron. *The University of Chicago Law Review*, 1159–1202.

Sweet, P. L. (2015). Chronic victims, risky women: Domestic violence advocacy and the medicalization of abuse. *Signs: Journal of Women in Culture and Society*, 41(1), 81–106.

Swinnen, J. (2015). Changing coalitions in value chains and the political economy of agricultural and food policy. *Oxford Review of Economic Policy*, 31(1), 90–115.

Switzer, J. V., & Vaughn, J. (1997). *Green Backlash: The History and Politics of the Environmental Opposition in the US*. Boulder, CO: Lynne Rienner Publishers.

Tarlock, A. D. (2012). United States flood control policy: The incomplete transition from the illusion of total protection to risk management. *Duke Environmental Law and Policy Forum*, 23, 151–184.

Taylor-Gooby, P. (2006). Social and public policy: Reflexive individualization and regulatory governance. In P. Taylor-Gooby & J. O. Zinn, eds., *Risk in Social Science*. Oxford: Oxford University Press, pp. 271–287.

Taylor-Gooby, P. (Ed.). (2004). *New Risks, New Welfare: The Transformation of the European Welfare State*. Oxford: Oxford University Press.

Temin, P. (1985). Government actions in times of crisis: Lessons from the history of drug regulation. *Journal of Social History*, 18(3), 433–438.

Thomas, C. I. (2014). *In Food We Trust: The Politics of Purity in American Food Regulation*. Lincoln: University of Nebraska Press.

Tierney, K. (2015). Resilience and the neoliberal project: Discourses, critiques, practices – and Katrina. *American Behavioral Scientist*, 59(10), 1327–1342.

Tilly, C. (1985). War making and state making as organized crime. In C. Besteman, ed., *Violence: A Reader*. New York: New York University Press, pp. 35–60.

Trein, P. (2018). *Healthy or Sick? Coevolution of Health Care and Public Health in a Comparative Perspective*. Cambridge: Cambridge University Press.

Trein, P. (2017). Coevolution of policy sectors: A comparative analysis of healthcare and public health. *Public Administration*, 95(3), 744–758.

Trentmann, F. (2004). Beyond consumerism: New historical perspectives on consumption. *Journal of Contemporary History*, 39(3), 373–401.

Tsoukala, A. (2006). Democracy in the light of security: British and French political discourses on domestic counter-terrorism policies. *Political Studies*, 54(3), 607–627.

Trumbull, G. (2012). *Strength in Numbers: The Political Power of Weak Interests*. Cambridge, MA: Harvard University Press.

Trumbull, G. (2006). *Consumer Capitalism: Politics, Product Markets, and Firm Strategy in France and Germany*. Ithaca, NY: Cornell University Press.

Tulchinsky, T. H., & Varavikova, E. A. (2014). *The New Public Health*. Cambridge, MA: Academic Press.

Tunstall, A. M., Weible, C. M., Tomsich, E. A., & Gover, A. R. (2016). Understanding policy reform in Colorado's domestic violence offender treatment standards. *Social Policy & Administration*, 50(5), 580–598.

Urofsky, M. I. (1985). State courts and protective legislation during the Progressive Era: A reevaluation. *The Journal of American History*, 72(1), 63–91.

Vardi, I. (2014). Quantifying accidents: Cars, statistics, and unintended consequences in the construction of social problems over time. *Qualitative Sociology*, 37(3), 345–367.

Vasterman, P., Yzermans, C. J., & Dirkzwager, A. J. (2005). The role of the media and media hypes in the aftermath of disasters. *Epidemiologic Reviews*, 27(1), 107–114.

Vogel, D. (2012). *The Politics of Precaution: Regulating Health, Safety, and Environmental Risks in Europe and the United States*. Princeton, NJ: Princeton University Press.

Vogel, D. (2009). *Trading Up: Consumer and Environmental Regulation in a Global Economy*. Cambridge, MA: Harvard University Press.

Vogel, D. (2003). The hare and the tortoise revisited: The new politics of consumer and environmental regulation in Europe. *British Journal of Political Science*, 33(4), 557–580.

Vogel, D. (1986). *National styles of regulation: Environmental Policy in Great Britain and the United States*. Ithaca, NY: Cornell University Press.

Vogel, S. K. (1998). *Freer Markets, More Rules: Regulatory Reform in Advanced Industrial Countries*. Ithaca, NY: Cornell University Press.

Wacquant, L. (2010). Crafting the neoliberal state: Workfare, prisonfare, and social insecurity. *Sociological Forum* 25 (2), 197–220.

Wacquant, L. (2009). *Punishing the Poor: The Neoliberal Government of Social Insecurity*. Durham: Duke University Press.

Wæver, O. (1995). Securitization and desecuritization. In R. Liphshutz, ed., *On Security*. New York: Columbia University Press.

Waldron, J. (2006). Safety and security. *Nebraska Law Review*, 85, 454–507.

Walker, B. A. (2010). Deciphering risk: Sex offender statutes and moral panic in a risk society. *University of Baltimore Law Review*, 40, 183–214.

Wälti, S. (2004). How multilevel structures affect environmental policy in industrialized countries. *European Journal of Political Research*, 43(4), 599–634.

Wang, J. (2005). Imagining the administrative state: Legal pragmatism, securities regulation, and New Deal liberalism. *Journal of Policy History*, 17(3), 257–293.

Wardman, J. K., & Löfstedt, R. (2018). Anticipating or accommodating to public concern? Risk amplification and the politics of precaution reexamined. *Risk Analysis*, 38(9), 1802–1819.

Weingart, P. (1999) Scientific expertise and political accountability: Paradoxes of science in politics. *Science and Public Policy* 26(3), 151–161.

Weitzer, R. (2007). The social construction of sex trafficking: Ideology and institutionalization of a moral crusade. *Politics & Society*, 35(3), 447–475.

Weldon, S. L., & Htun, M. (2013). Feminist mobilisation and progressive policy change: Why governments take action to combat violence against women. *Gender & Development*, 21(2), 231 247.

Welsh, B. C., Braga, A. A., & Sullivan, C. J. (2014). Serious youth violence and innovative prevention: On the emerging link between public health and criminology. *Justice Quarterly*, 31(3), 500–523.

Whitman, J. Q. (2007). Consumerism versus producerism: A study in comparative law. *Yale Law Journal*, 117, 340–407.

Wiener, J. B., & Rogers, M. D. (2002). Comparing precaution in the United States and Europe. *Journal of Risk Research*, 5(4), 317–349.

Wikander, U., Kessler-Harris, A., & Lewis, J. E. (Eds.). (1995). *Protecting Women: Labor Legislation in Europe, the United States, and Australia, 1880–1920*. Champaign: University of Illinois Press.

Wiktorowicz, M. E. (2003). Emergent patterns in the regulation of pharmaceuticals: Institutions and interests in the United States, Canada, Britain, and France. *Journal of Health Politics, Policy and Law*, 28(4), 615–658.

Wiley, L. F., Berman, M. L., & Blanke, D. (2013). Who's Your Nanny? Choice, paternalism and public health in the age of personal responsibility. *The Journal of Law, Medicine & Ethics*, 41, 88–91.

Williams, M. C. (2011). Securitization and the liberalism of fear. *Security Dialogue*, 42(4–5), 453–463.

Wilson, G. K. (1985). *The Politics of Safety and Health: Occupational Safety and Health in the United States and Britain*. Oxford: Oxford University Press.

Wilson, J. Q. (1980). *The Politics of Regulation*. New York: Basic Books.

Wolfe, M. (2012). Putting on the brakes or pressing on the gas? Media attention and the speed of policymaking. *Policy Studies Journal*, 40(1), 109–126.

Woloch, N. (2015). *A Class by Herself: Protective Laws for Women Workers, 1890s–1990s*. Princeton, NJ: Princeton University Press.

Wood, D. B., & Doan, A. (2003). The politics of problem definition: Applying and testing threshold models. *American Journal of Political Science*, 47(4), 640–653.

Wood, D. M. (2007). Beyond the panopticon? Foucault and surveillance studies. In S. Elden, ed., *Space, Knowledge and Power: Foucault and Geography*. Abingdon: Routledge, pp. 245–263.

Wood, M. (2016). Paradoxical politics: Emergency, security and the depoliticisation of flooding. *Political Studies*, 64(3), 699–718.

Wood, R. S. (2006). Tobacco's tipping point: The Master Settlement Agreement as a focusing event. *Policy Studies Journal*, 34(3), 419–436.

Wuthnow, R. (2010). *Be Very Afraid: The Cultural Response to Terror, Pandemics, Environmental Devastation, Nuclear Annihilation, and Other Threats*. Oxford: Oxford University Press.

Wynne, B. (2001). Creating public alienation: Expert cultures of risk and ethics on GMOs. *Science as Culture*, 10(4), 445–481.

Yamaguchi, T. (2014). Social imaginary and dilemmas of policy practice: The food safety arena in Japan. *Food Policy*, 45, 167–173.

Acknowledgments

Although this Element is short, the ideas expressed came together over a long period of time. My earliest interest in the themes that grew into this Element stretch back to a project with David Vogel that investigated the challenge that the European Union and its member states confronted in dealing with issues like mad cow disease and genetically modified foods. A short follow-on project with Jane Gingrich on how the British state responded to the mad cow crisis brought home the challenge that public institutions face in handling novel, fast-moving risks. To explore these issues further, I did a study of an international infectious disease response network (GOARN) with Egbert Sondorp and Robert Hartley Stevens, which later evolved into a National Science Foundation study co-directed with Ann Keller and Art Reingold. This research led, in turn, to work with Arjen Boin and Martin Bartenberger on crisis management and to further projects on food safety with John Yasuda, food safety and child protection with Patrick Baur, toxic chemicals regulation with Jörg Balsiger, and HIV/AIDS prevention with Gabrielle Goldstein. Most recently, an edited book project with Jarle Trondal and Morten Øgård, *Governance in Turbulent Times*, deepened my understanding of what I now call "unruly problems."

Through this work, I began to glimpse the wider "politics of protection" that developed into the main theme of this book. A special note of thanks to Berkeley undergraduate students in my *Public Administration* and *Public Problems* classes, where I explored some of these issues. Thanks also to the students who took my graduate seminars on risk and regulation and comparative public policy. I also greatly appreciate the help of the Cambridge Elements editors.

Along the way, a number of friends and family from near and far (beyond those noted earlier) have contributed to the project, including Eric Baekkeskov, Mathilde Bourrier, Margaretha Breese, Sahai Burrowes, Dan Carpenter, Tom Christensen, Can Ciner, Louise Comfort, Salo Coslovsky, Moshe Farjoun, Robert Geyer, Mark Hunter, Sanneke Kuipers, Per Lægreid, Todd LaPorte, Theresa MacPhail, Satoshi Miura, PerOla Öberg, Charles Parker, Paul Pierson, Konrad Posch, Mark Rhinard, Al Roberts, Phil Rocco, Emery Roe, Bill Ryan, Suzanne Ryan, Lise Ryykja, Paul Schulman, Eva Sørensen, Matthew Stenberg, Paul 't Hart, Jacob Torfing, Philipp Trein and Steve Vogel. May the state protect you!

Cambridge Elements ≡

Public Policy

M. Ramesh

National University of Singapore (NUS)

M. Ramesh is UNESCO Chair on Social Policy Design at the Lee Kuan Yew School of Public Policy, NUS. His research focuses on governance and social policy in East and Southeast Asia, in addition to public policy institutions and processes. He has published extensively in reputed international journals. He is co-editor of Policy and Society and Policy Design and Practice.

Michael Howlett

Simon Fraser University, British Colombia

Michael Howlett is Burnaby Mountain Professor and Canada Research Chair (Tier 1) in the Department of Political Science, Simon Fraser University. He specializes in public policy analysis, and resource and environmental policy. He is currently editor-in-chief of *Policy Sciences* and co-editor of the *Journal of Comparative Policy Analysis, Policy and Society,* and *Policy Design and Practice.*

David L. Weimer

University of Wisconsin–Madison

David L. Weimer is the Edwin E. Witte Professor of Political Economy, University of Wisconsin–Madison. He has a long-standing interest in policy craft and has conducted policy research in the areas of energy, criminal justice, and health policy. In 2013 he served as president of the Society for Benefit-Cost Analysis. He is a fellow of the National Academy of Public Administration.

Xun WU

Hong Kong University of Science and Technology

Xun Wu is Professor and Head of the Division of Public Policy at the Hong Kong University of Science and Technology. He is a policy scientist whose research interests include policy innovations, water resource management, and health policy reform. He has been involved extensively in consultancy and executive education, his work involving consultations for the World Bank and UNEP.

Judith Clifton

University of Cantabria

Judith Clifton is Professor of Economics at the University of Cantabria, Spain. She has published in leading policy journals and is editor-in-chief of the *Journal of Economic Policy Reform.* Most recently, her research enquires how emerging technologies can transform public administration, a forward-looking cutting-edge project that received €3.5 million funding from the Horizon2020 program.

Eduardo Araral

National University of Singapore (NUS)

Eduardo Araral is widely published in various journals and books and has presented in forty conferences. He is currently co-director of the Institute of Water Policy at the Lee Kuan Yew School of Public Policy, NUS and is a member of the editorial board of *Journal of Public Administration Research and Theory* and the board of the Public Management Research Association.

About the series

This series is a collection of assessments in the future of public policy research as well as substantive new research.
Edited by leading scholars in the field, the series is an ideal medium for reflecting on and advancing the understanding of critical issues in the public sphere. Collectively, the series provides a forum for broad and diverse coverage of all major topics in the field while integrating different disciplinary and methodological approaches.

Public Policy

Printed in the United States
By Bookmasters